Praise for *Love Me in the Waiting*

Increasingly, we have come to expect everything in an instant. Vaccine production that once took a decade is now delivered at "warp speed." Our favorite TV shows and films are now delivered to us "on demand" in the comfort and convenience of our own homes. Fast-food restaurants deliver our meals to us in less than a minute. At home, we have the options of instant rice, instant oatmeal, instant grits, with Instant Pots and microwaves to assist. Our handheld devices deliver breaking news from home and abroad . . . instantly. The instantness of almost everything has, for Christians especially, caused many to devalue the centuries-long virtue of delayed gratification through waiting. Even the greatest saints of scripture did not receive all the promises in their lifetimes, because they were looking toward a "better country" whose architect and builder is God. In their waiting, and precisely because of their waiting, they found fertile soil that satisfied them *in* their waiting—soil that connected them to the source of joy Himself, who is Jesus Christ. Krystal does a wonderful job helping us reconnect with this soil.

Scott Sauls, senior pastor of
Christ Presbyterian Church in
Nashville, Tennessee, and author of
several books, including *Jesus Outside
the Lines* and *A Gentle Answer*

Our days are filled with moments that sometimes compile into long waiting periods. Now, more than ever, people are experiencing the world at a slower pace. Waiting for our lives to "go back to normal" has been an unwelcomed definition of what truly waiting looks like. In *Love Me in the Waiting*, Krystal explores the why of the waiting and how we can wait, not only better, but more successfully than we ever have. The Bible gives us a great guidebook on how to wait well if we choose to see it that way. Do yourself a favor and dive into these words of wisdom to help you navigate uncertain seas in your life.

Mark Batterson, lead pastor of National
Community Church in Washington, DC, and
New York Times best-selling
author of *The Circle Maker*

Waiting. It's not my favorite thing; most of us would say the same. What do we do when we're doing all we can and we still find ourselves waiting? Waiting for opportunity, waiting for healing, waiting for breakthrough, waiting for some sign that it won't always be this way . . . waiting can be taxing and deflating, and can even cause us to doubt things we thought we knew about God. Krystal shows us in *Love Me in the Waiting* that the waiting seasons are not without purpose. God wants us whole and He wants us free, and He'll often take us on a journey of discovery before we get to the fulfillment of what we hope for. God has your back and He wants what is best for you. Krystal's book is a timely encouragement that God is for us and will not forsake us, even in the middle of the most trying times.

Dave Dummitt, senior pastor of Willow Creek Community Church in South Barrington, Illinois

LOVE
ME
IN
THE
WAITING

Krystal Ribble

LOVE
ME
IN
THE
WAITING

Trusting God's Purpose When
You're Longing for What's Next

DEXTERITY
NASHVILLE

Dexterity, LLC
604 Magnolia Lane
Nashville, TN 37211

Printed in the United States of America.

First edition: 2021
10 9 8 7 6 5 4 3 2 1

ISBN: 978-1-947297-25-8 (trade paper)
ISBN: 978-1-947297-26-5 (eBook)

Publisher's Cataloging-in-Publication data

Names: Ribble, Krystal, author.
Title: Love me in the waiting : trusting God's purpose when you're longing for what's next / written by Krystal Ribble.
Description: Nashville, TN: Dexterity, 2021.
Identifiers: ISBN: 9781947297258 (paperback) | 9781947297265 (ebook)
Subjects: LCSH Trust in God—Christianity. | Expectation (Psychology)—Religious aspects—Christianity. | Waiting (Philosophy) | Hope—Religious aspects—Christianity. | Christian living. | BISAC RELIGION / Christian Living / Personal Growth | RELIGION / Christian Living / Spiritual Growth | SELF-HELP / Personal Growth / Happiness
Classification: LCC BV4637 .R54 2021 | DDC 248.1/4–dc23

Book design by PerfecType.
Cover design by twoline || STUDIO.

DEDICATION

For my parents, Tom and Brenda Tucker,
who continually live out a steadiness of trust in the Lord
and unwavering faith in whatever
seasons the Lord brings their way.
Your firm foundation has helped me navigate many
uncertain circumstances with much more
ease and prayerful hope than I could have ever imagined.
Thank you for waiting on the Lord and
showing me how to as well.
I love you both so much.

It is taking everything within me to keep waiting, but this is the miracle I am coming to know: this desert journey has made me weary but my heart is still slouched toward hope. And I will believe I can know peace without knowing what comes next. I will trust that in the waiting everything connects. Today is not in vain. and I will grow and I will change in beautiful, meaningful ways.

my heart
is slouched
toward hope

—Morgan Harper Nichols,
artist, poet, and musician[1]

CONTENTS

FOREWORD

When God told Abram that he would be the father of a great nation, Abram didn't have a single heir. Not one. But it wasn't for a lack of trying. He and his wife Sarai had discovered over the long tenure of their marriage that they were unable to conceive. They were barren.

And yet, God had made a promise—one that set them off on a long journey away from their home to a place the Lord said He would show them once they got there. God told them that their descendants would bless the entire world and that they would be many. How many? The Lord took Abram out into the night of the desert sky and said, "Count the stars."

Have you ever seen a desert sky at night? The canopy of stars stretches from horizon to horizon, so vast, so deep, so numerous, and so *old*. To look into the starry night is to look back into time.

I remember being in a desert under the light of the last sliver of a waning moon, whose light cast shadows as though it was day. We didn't need headlamps to see where we were going. The glory of the heavens lit the way as we walked.

I think about that when I think about God's promise to Abram to make him the father of a great nation, because it was a promise that had yet to come true, and from Abram and Sarai's perspective, the *means* by which it could come to pass at all was an even greater mystery than *when*. So God showed him the stars. He showed His earthbound servant, bound by time, ancient lights fixed in the heavens and said, "Your descendants will be like this."

It isn't the volume of stars that moves me most about that story. It's that when Abram struggled to comprehend how God was going to do the seemingly impossible, God didn't just show him stars. He showed Abram *glory*—breathtaking, wonder-filled, otherworldly glory. This was how the Lord bolstered Abram's faith during the waiting—not so much by explaining His plan, but by revealing His glory.

We wait. For big and small things, for important and mundane things, for vision-propelling and dream-crushing things, we wait. That is nothing new, is it? And yet we, like every generation that has come before, struggle in the waiting. We wonder if we're fools to hope. If we're strong enough to endure possible disappointment. If God can restore what seems so utterly lost to us. We're like Abram and Sarai—we look at the world through the lenses we've been given, and sometimes what we see offers no conceivable way forward.

But God took Abram out to see the stars—the glorious, infinite evidence of His power and authority over time, there on display for us to see every night of our lives. As sailors use them to navigate the sea, God gave them to Abram to help him navigate his hope and fear.

The God we wait on has not changed. The Maker of the stars who opened Sarai's womb, creating a covenant lineage that would lead through Abraham, Isaac, Jacob, and Joseph to David and Solomon, and all the way to Christ Himself, calls us to walk roads where we can't see what lies around the bend. So we must learn the art of trusting Him.

How do we do that? By going to the Word He gave us, which is filled with stories of God leading His people through things we all experience, beautifully explored in this book—forgiveness, relational complexity, questions about the future, fears of sickness and death, a hunger for all to be put right.

As you read *Love Me in the Waiting*, ask God to give you more than mere information. Ask Him to reveal His glory, because that is where His love, power, and perfection converge. If you are a follower of Jesus, this intersection is where you reside all the time, whether you feel that way or not. The One who keeps you is faithful. If you don't believe it would be accurate to identify yourself as a Christian, but you are curious about the faith in which this book is anchored, by all means, pray the same prayer. Ask God to reveal His glory to you in the fragility of your waiting, because here's the truth this book will help you see—though things may seem fragile to you, to God they are not.

Russ Ramsey, pastor of Christ Presbyterian Church, Cool Springs in Nashville, Tennessee, and author of *Struck* and the Retelling the Story series
February 5, 2021

INTRODUCTION

WORDS FOR
The Waiting

I believe that I shall look upon the goodness of the LORD
    in the land of the living!
Wait for the LORD;
    be strong, and let your heart take courage;
    wait for the LORD!

—Psalm 27:13–14

If you are reading this, I know you have experienced at least one massive waiting period in life, because as I write, the entire world is entrapped in a global pandemic. When will it end? When will there be a vaccine? When can my kids go back to school? Will my office ever open back up? Will we always have to wear masks in public? These are just a few of the questions I am sure have been swirling around in people's minds. I can say with certainty, you will go through multiple waiting periods in your lifetime.

Currently, my little family finds itself in an intense season of waiting—the pandemic of 2020 carries on, and I am suspended between weekly chemo appointments for my oldest son. In fact, many of the words you will read in this book were penned as I sat next to my son while he received his treatments. The timing has been both ironic and wonderful, how God has me writing about waiting while I am literally waiting on multiple things.

Even though we have known for some time that our son would one day need chemo due to the side effects of his neurological disease, the news that it was time to start treatment wasn't an easy pill to swallow.

So here I am, *waiting*. Waiting on his healing.

While we have an "end" to this first chemo round, there is no end to his disease. There is no cure. While my human mind waits for the healing to happen, I do so with the image of an "end." This is what we all do. It's how we all cope. We all hope for the "end" of whatever has us frozen in time. You see, *everyone* is waiting for something. In our society, our lives, our economy, our reality—we are all waiting. If you aren't currently waiting for something or someone, you have at some point in your life, or you will be soon.

We wait for our troubled times to pass. We wait to one day meet our soul mate. We wait to have children. We wait on those around us to make better decisions. We wait for reconciliation and restored relationships. We wait on the Lord to hear us and answer our prayers.

Essentially, we are always waiting for the grass to be greener and the sky to be clearer.

But what if our waiting was always purposeful? What if God's plan all along was made better by our seasons of waiting? What if our waiting led us to the paradise of abundant life? What if our waiting was not in fact *taking* something from us, but *giving* us more than we have asked or dreamed? And what if our waiting isn't leading us to an end, but to Jesus?

This book explores the different ways God shows up in your waiting seasons and what He may want to show you during that unique time. We will explore stories in the Bible of people who waited for many different things to come to fruition. Our journey will take us from Genesis all the way to John. Although the people in the Bible can seem removed from us because they lived long before us, I propose to you that our waiting seasons are quite similar, and as we'll see when we dive into modern examples of waiting, God's lessons apply universally, without fail.

INTRODUCTION

My hope is that through each story we encounter, you are able to feel God's love and trust that He has purpose in your waiting seasons. He is there, and His will is drenched in promise for you. The Lord is doing a lot in your waiting seasons, and given the right mindset, you can see how He is using this time. Some of the concepts we'll explore are how He has purpose, how He is preserving who you are, how He provides abundantly, and how you can always expect Him to show up.

Within each period of waiting we study, we look at how God was present in those times and what He has done for us today. Join me, friend, on the journey you never thought you wanted to go on.

ONE

Waiting FOR THE STORM TO PASS

Dear Noah,

We could have sworn you said the ark wasn't leaving till 5.

Sincerely,
The Unicorns

—*As seen on a greeting card*

The dead of night. Two little ones asleep in their beds. News alerts blaring on the cell phones that a tornado was headed straight for the house. Hurriedly scooping up children and rushing downstairs. Hunkering down, hearing wind gusting in and out, crashing thunder all around, walls ripping and objects flying. Covering the children's heads and huddling together.

Then . . . silence.

Deafening silence. You stand up, you grab the children, you open the door to see what damage was done. Dust, splintered wood, broken glass, ripped furniture, toys and books everywhere. Your whole home turned upside down in a matter of minutes.

The storm may have passed, but you still have to live in the aftermath. Just because the storm has passed doesn't mean the damage has disappeared.

I'm describing a literal storm. A storm much like one some of our closest friends went through in our hometown of Nashville, Tennessee. They lost their home and their cars. Their two little children were uprooted, and they started over as a family.

For me, on the other side of town, the storm had passed, and I did not feel or lose a thing. For them, the storm had passed and wreaked havoc on their whole lives. We both woke up the next day to very different realities, even though we were only separated by ten miles.

You may have experienced a storm like this. Every year in the United States, tornadoes create about $400 million worth of damage and take around seventy lives with them.[2] With around 328 million people in the United

States, that number of seventy is only a tiny, tiny drop in the bucket of the US population.

But what about the other kinds of storms? How many people are affected by other storms that suspended them into a time of waiting? The emotional storms, the physical storms, the storms that leave a wake in their souls? I would dare say that of the 328 million people in our country, most would raise their hands in agreement for having endured this kind of storm.

What happens when the storms hit us, and how do we deal with the aftermath of the waiting? In what position should our hearts continually be so that when the storm rages, we aren't left so destitute? When we step out from under the shelter and climb through the rubble, what purpose can we find?

The most famous literal storm in the Bible happened with a man named Noah, and while his situation seemed completely unreal and certainly bleak, his story is dripping with purpose. We find him in Genesis 6 as a man God favored. Everyone else on earth was making God sick (for real, read Genesis 6:5–8).

From day one of knowing about the storm all the way to the end of the wreckage, Noah's story is full of promises and gems the Lord left him. And that Noah . . . what a stand-up guy. His perspective colored the entire experience for him, his family, and for generations to come. His blind faith and belief in the goodness of God carried him through the largest natural disaster the world would ever see—a flood that covered the whole earth.

We've never seen this again. We may have seen flooding in certain areas and know people who have lost things or perished in that type of disaster, but the whole earth covered in water at one time? Never again has it happened. And we have a promise that He will never do this again.

But let's back up a little. Let's dive into Noah's story while seeing the parallel here in our modern-day world. In the end, we will get to that promise.

God's Purpose in the Storm

Storms, literal and emotional, can be both imminent and surprising. Sometimes you know they are coming, and other times, they pop up on top of you. My friends in Nashville had some warning about their literal storm. Though there was no way to prepare to completely miss the storm, they knew it was headed their way and were able to hunker down to survive it. We will see in a little bit that this was also true of Noah: he knew what was coming and prepared to survive—not miss—it.

Other times, though, you have no warning. The call that a young loved one has been tragically killed. The conversation where your spouse admits they want to leave you. The meeting where you find out you don't have a job anymore. These are sudden, breathtaking reminders that life can turn on a dime.

When the storm is looming, being uncertain and scared are natural tendencies. When my friends knew a tornado was headed for their home, fear and anxiety ran rampant. They had two children to consider and didn't know if their home or possessions would survive. When you are suddenly hit with emotional turmoil—be it family drama, a divorce, lost friendships, a child getting cancer, a loved one dying—you sometimes can't see the storm coming.

The storms we navigate today, that propel us into all kinds of waiting seasons, are not much unlike the storms of Noah's day. Though our storms might not compare on a physical level to his, the parallels between what the Lord taught Noah and what He is teaching us are uncanny.

Noah had a warning. God came to him and told him what He was planning to do and how Noah and his whole family would be able to survive. We learn the details from Genesis:

Now the earth was corrupt in God's sight, and the earth was filled with violence. And God saw the earth, and behold, it was corrupt, for all flesh had corrupted their way on the earth. And God said to Noah, "I have determined to make an end of all flesh, for the earth is filled with violence through them. Behold, I will destroy them with the earth. Make yourself an ark of gopher wood. Make rooms in the ark, and cover it inside and out with pitch. This is how you are to make it: the length of the ark 300 cubits, its breadth 50 cubits, and its height 30 cubits. Make a roof for the ark, and finish it to a cubit above, and set the door of the ark in its side. Make it with lower, second, and third decks. For behold, I will bring a flood of waters upon the earth to destroy all flesh in which is the breath of life under heaven. Everything that is on the earth shall die. But I will establish my covenant with you, and you shall come into the ark, you, your sons, your wife, and your sons' wives with you. And of every living thing of all flesh, you shall bring two of every sort into the ark to keep them alive with you. They shall be male and female. Of the birds according to their kinds, and of the animals according to their kinds, of every creeping thing of the ground, according to its kind, two of every sort shall come in to you to keep them alive. Also take with you every sort of food that is eaten, and store it up. It shall serve as food for you and for them." Noah did this; he did all that God commanded him.

(Genesis 6:11–22)

What I love about the Lord is that no matter whether you have a warning of the storm or not, His purpose for you and *who He is* remain the same. How well you navigate the panicked waters and how successfully you stand up from the wreckage are big deals to Him. He wants success for you, and He wants an abundant life in your future.

God says in verse 19 that His provision for Noah would keep all the animals and Noah's family "alive with you." This was more than a promise that they wouldn't die, this was a promise that *when they survived the storm, there was life on the other side.*

I can't imagine being locked up in a boat, with a million animals, knowing the whole earth as you knew it was under water. Would there be any doubt while you were in the ark as to whether God's promises would be true? I imagine myself huddling in a corner of the ark, shaking while covering my ears to drown out the mooing. I wouldn't have been a good shipmate.

Be honest, when God takes you through a storm of any kind, do you find yourself doubting Him in the middle of the swirling winds and crashing emotions? I sometimes really wonder if He knows what He's doing. I mean, His track record is impeccable, yet I *still* question if He knows what's best for me. Because this storm, this doesn't seem like a great idea.

However, here we have Noah, being called to wait out the biggest storm in history. And the guy does *exactly* what God asks of him. The Bible shows Noah as a positive guy whom the Lord loved. It appears Noah just blindly followed His leading, but we know this could not have been an easy pill to swallow.

Just picture Noah's wife! Goodness. I can't imagine it was the easiest thing in the world to say, "Yes, honey, I will go live in this boat with you and our whole family and two of every animal while the whole earth is destroyed. I trust this is a great decision." Maybe she was a lot better than me—and I am sure she was—but I would have looked at my husband sideways and said, "When did you hit your head? Please come with me to the doctor right now."

I mean honestly, can you imagine being locked up with your entire family and a bunch of animals in a boat while the whole earth is being destroyed? Can you imagine *not* wanting to kill everyone inside? I would have perished in that storm. My doubt and my impatience would have sunk me.

God's purpose in this storm was multifaceted, but the one purpose I want you to see was His purpose in saving Noah and his family. The Lord wanted safety and a future for Noah. In the middle of a trial or a storm, we seldom think God is positioning for our safety. However, friend, our safety is paramount to Him.

> In the middle of a trial or a storm, we seldom think God is positioning for our safety. However, friend, our safety is paramount to Him.

How you navigate that emotional trial is of utmost importance to Him. Your safety through the storm is what leads you to the life He has for you. *Your safety is paramount.* Don't forget this.

God Preserves Who You Are

When we enter a waiting period of life, we can almost feel like time stands still. It's as if the Lord has hit a pause button and is keeping us suspended in time. I say this because there have been times when He has brought me to what I felt was a "holding" place while everyone around me continued to move on. Their lives kept going, and I was going to have a lot of catching up to do. This feeling happens no matter if the waiting period is sudden or anticipated, whether it comes harshly or creeps in quietly. No matter how we are asked to wait on God, this time period can make us feel like the world is carrying on without us.

For Noah, the world was literally drowning around him. He wasn't missing out on anything important, and he certainly didn't wish he were outside the ark rather than inside it. Imagine if you felt the same way, that you would *rather* be waiting. Wouldn't you rather be waiting in a season the Lord prepared for you, rather than moving on in a season He did not create for you?

Genesis 7 tells us about when the flood came upon the earth and how God preserved Noah and his family, and all the animals of the land, inside the ark. In verse 1, He tells Noah, "Go into the ark, you and all your household, for I have seen that you are righteous before me in this generation."

And then we learn in verses 6–13 how Noah carried out God's instructions:

Noah was six hundred years old when the flood of waters came upon the earth. And Noah and his sons and his wife and his sons' wives with him went into the ark to escape the waters of the flood. Of clean animals, and of animals that are not clean, and of birds, and of everything that creeps on the ground, two and two, male and female, went into the ark with Noah, as God had commanded Noah. And after seven days the waters of the flood came upon the earth.

In the six hundredth year of Noah's life, in the second month, on the seventeenth day of the month, on that day all the fountains of the great deep burst forth, and the windows of the heavens were opened. And rain fell upon the earth forty days and forty nights. On the very same day Noah and his sons, Shem and Ham and Japheth, and Noah's wife and the three wives of his sons with them entered the ark.

You may read this story and think, *Great, Noah knew the storm was coming, and God prepared a way for him to save himself. How does this apply to me when I had no fair warning He was going to suspend me in time with this waiting period?*

My friends who lost everything in the Nashville tornado felt alone in their experiences. Except for a few friends on their street, no one else in their circle of influence could relate to what they were going through. As I mentioned before, the storm passed and on the other side of town,

I went about the next day as if nothing had happened. But my friends still didn't have a home, or cars, or any of the possessions they'd had twenty-four hours earlier. For them, time stood still, just as I imagine it did in the ark.

You enter a season of waiting with the remembrance of what was. However, when you emerge from this season, things will not be as they were. What if while the whole world moves on, the Lord is keeping you in a season of suspension to preserve you? Read what Genesis says next:

> *They went into the ark with Noah, two and two of all flesh in which there was the breath of life. And those that entered, male and female of all flesh, went in as God had commanded him. And the LORD shut him in.*
>
> *(Genesis 7:15–16)*

The detail this scripture gives us of "the Lord shut him in" is of utmost importance to understanding His preservation. This verse is referring to the closing of the ark door and how *God shut the door*, not Noah. This is a reminder that God preserves those He saves. Noah had no say on when the ark door would close or when the storms would start. Noah did not decide any of this, just as we do not decide when storms will hit and how/if we will be saved from them. The ark shows us Who is in charge of the winds and the waves and Who decides to save us.

God loved who Noah was. He wanted Noah's demeanor and faith to live on for generations to come, but He knew the rest of the earth needed a pruning that someone as wonderful as Noah wouldn't be able to survive. So, He created a way for Noah to be preserved during such an incredible storm.

What if your storm is preserving you? What if your storm is suspending you in time because of who you are and the parts of you God wants to keep safe?

> What if your storm is preserving you? What if your storm is suspending you in time because of who you are and the parts of you God wants to keep safe?

You may not feel that way right now. If a literal storm is raging around you and you are losing all this world has offered you, just maybe the Lord is trying to show you that no earthly possessions can sustain you; He is the only thing you need. If an emotional storm is engulfing you, ripping away relationships or desires you have long held dear, maybe He is wanting to preserve who you are currently by not allowing these relationships or circumstances to change you.

The other side of your storm needs who you are right now. Had you tried to fight this storm, you would have lost who you are. If Noah thought the Lord had lost His mind and didn't follow His leading, he would have perished along with all the animals and every other person on this earth. And quite frankly—you wouldn't be reading these words right now. Imagine that. Because God preserved Noah, you are here.

God's Perfect Peace

Talking about peace and storms within the same conversation illustrates quite the paradox. These things do not seem to coexist. But if anyone can teach us about peace in the midst of a storm, it's Noah. His steadiness carried his family, all the animals, and even us now, through the largest storm in history. No wonder God chose him.

Every time I talk about peace, the truth in Isaiah 26:3 rings loudly no matter what waiting period I'm in. This verse says, "You keep him in perfect peace whose mind is stayed on you, because he trusts in you." God wants peace for you. His goal truly is always to keep you at peace, especially when the storms threaten your serenity. Take a lesson from Noah—keep your mind on the Lord, and you will have peace.

I can't imagine every day inside the ark was peaceful. The Bible doesn't say that when they entered the ark, He shut everyone's mouth. Lord knows if everyone could still talk or squawk or neigh or bark, there was not a lot of peace happening. The same goes for our storms.

When my friends were in the middle of a tornado, it was loud. The damage happening all around them may have occurred in the dead of night, but it didn't happen quietly. Although their continued wreckage seemed silent to some, the reminders of all they had to do to rebuild was, at times, deafening to them.

The same can be said of emotional storms. What seems silent on the outside to some feels and sounds like hurricane winds in the hearts and minds of those waiting for the storm to pass.

They say the eye of a tornado is eerily quiet. Everything around the eye is causing mass destruction, but the center of the storm is calm. Apply this to your storm. While the winds may be raging and wreaking havoc on ideals, relationships, or physical things you hold dear, the calmest place to be in the storm is right in the middle of it. We wouldn't ordinarily wish to be right smack dab in the middle of our storm, but if that's where we are safest, if that's where peace abounds, that is where I want to be.

The storms the Lord allows us to go through are not things we can avoid. What we do have control over, however, are our attitudes within them. For Noah, this was the exact thing that carried him through. The Bible does not elaborate on Noah's mindset, but it does show us on two occasions some important truths about Noah:

Noah did this; he did all that God commanded him.
(Genesis 6:22)

And Noah did all that the LORD had commanded him.
(Genesis 7:5)

When you do as God has led, and there is no surrounding commentary, you have peace in your heart about what He is asking of you.

We don't know all the other thoughts Noah had. Noah was a human, like we are. Even though he found favor in God, he was not God himself, so his life wasn't without blemish. However, despite any private thoughts or quiet conversations of doubt he may have had with his family, his heart's ultimate position was obedience, and this laid the foundation for his entire peace in the midst of turmoil. He was certain. He was steady. He was a peaceful man in the midst of the largest storm in history.

The Lord longs to give you a firm foundation of steadiness. He longs to give you unwavering peace. Position your heart to receive the peace that comes with His presence.

For many of us, we can finally believe the goodness of God and the protection He brings once our feet are again on dry land. How would your attitude about your storm be different if you believed these things about God *before* the storm was over?

> The Lord longs to give you a firm foundation of steadiness. He longs to give you unwavering peace. Position your heart to receive the peace that comes with His presence.

Noah believed in the goodness of God and took confidence in His guiding protection because his attitude was fixed toward trust and peace. He waited on God's timing, and through his waiting, God showed up in mighty ways.

And about that promise? After the flood ceased, the Bible tells us what happened next:

> *Then Noah built an altar to the LORD and took some of every clean animal and some of every clean bird and offered burnt offerings on the altar. And when*

the LORD smelled the pleasing aroma, the LORD said in his heart, "I will never again curse the ground because of man, for the intention of man's heart is evil from his youth. Neither will I ever again strike down every living creature as I have done. While the earth remains, seedtime and harvest, cold and heat, summer and winter, day and night, shall not cease."

And God blessed Noah and his sons and said to them, "Be fruitful and multiply and fill the earth. The fear of you and the dread of you shall be upon every beast of the earth and upon every bird of the heavens, upon everything that creeps on the ground and all the fish of the sea. Into your hand they are delivered. Every moving thing that lives shall be food for you. And as I gave you the green plants, I give you everything."

(Genesis 8:20–9:3)

The Lord wanted Noah's family to multiply on the earth. Then every other living thing He had created was given to Noah and his descendants. What opulence to receive from the King of Kings! He saw so much favor in Noah and his family that after preserving them through this storm, He gave them so much in abundance.

Friend, take heart that the storm will cease, and you will come out better than when it began. God has given you the tools to navigate the wreckage from the waiting, you only need to believe in Him and His strength within you and stand up.

Or in Noah's case, open the window:

At the end of forty days Noah opened the window of the ark that he had made and sent forth a raven. It went to and fro until the waters were dried up from the earth. Then he sent forth a dove from him, to see if the waters had subsided from the face of the ground. But the dove found no place to set her foot, and she returned to him to the ark, for the waters were still on the face of the whole earth. So he put out his hand and took her and brought her into the ark with him. He waited another seven days, and again he sent forth the dove out of the ark. And the dove came back to him in the evening, and behold, in her mouth was a freshly plucked olive leaf. So Noah knew that the waters had subsided from the earth. Then he waited another seven days and sent forth the dove, and she did not return to him anymore.

(Genesis 8:6–12)

Noah opened the window that had blocked the storm from overtaking him. With curiosity, he sent the raven and the dove out to see if the birds could find the Lord's promise of dry land. The dove came back to him when she couldn't find a safe place to land. It wasn't time yet. While the literal storm was over, the emotional storm raged on—the safety of dry land was still not available.

Think about your storm. When it ceased, you didn't immediately go back to business as usual. It takes time to get back to a solid foundation in life. *Do not rush this process.*

Noah sent the dove out seven days later, and she came back with a leaf from an olive tree. God was showing Noah that not only was it safe to come out to dry land again, but He was also proving to Noah that He came to give him peace and friendship and victory. And as you probably know, this specific tree now holds the meaning of peace, friendship, and victory.

God has come to give you all the same things *in and through* your storm. Find Him in the winds *and* the rain. Stay where He is; He is your peace.

TWO

Waiting FOR NEW LIFE

Heaven blew every trumpet
and played every horn
on the wonderful, marvelous
night you were born.
   —*Nancy Tillman,* On the Night You Were Born[3]

When I was in the fourth grade, we lived in a tiny town in South Carolina. My teacher at the local elementary school owned a farm where she and her family occasionally bred and sold horses. Her son was my age, and some afternoons I would spend time at their house climbing the hay bales in the barns and riding the horses. I'm incredibly allergic to hay, so this was a tragic idea on my part, but there was a majesty to the horses I had not yet experienced in my short life. The power of them, coupled with the gentleness they showed my tiny nine-year-old self, intrigued me.

One afternoon, I ended up staying a little later than usual, and my teacher mentioned one of their horses was likely giving birth that night. I was fraught with anticipation. I had a hard time deciding whether to watch or if the fear of passing out would take over. Could my stomach handle the sight? My curiosity won, and I stood behind a fence as I watched my teacher and her husband help deliver the colt.

The moment was much quieter than I could have ever imagined. A reverence for the magnitude of what was happening permeated the air, and the night was so still. I stood transfixed. One moment this horse was pregnant, and the next, this tiny colt lay on the ground next to her. The only moments in my life that would ever rival this would be the three times I got to hold my children for the first time.

There is something about new life. Something intoxicating. The first cry of a newborn baby. The first chirp of a tiny bird. The tiny bud of promise on a flower stem. The moment of change in someone's heart.

Life comes in a million forms, and though we do not all recognize every moment, we are drawn to new life. In fact, we bend toward creating it. We could look at a lot of stories in the Bible that illustrate this, but the most prominent is the lifelong desire of Abraham and Sarah to create life.

We find their story in Genesis:

And God said to Abraham, "As for Sarai your wife, you shall not call her name Sarai, but Sarah shall be her name. I will bless her, and moreover, I will give you a son by her. I will bless her, and she shall become nations; kings of peoples shall come from her." Then Abraham fell on his face and laughed and said to himself, "Shall a child be born to a man who is a hundred years old? Shall Sarah, who is ninety years old, bear a child?" And Abraham said to God, "Oh that Ishmael might live before you!" God said, "No, but Sarah your wife shall bear you a son, and you shall call his name Isaac. I will establish my covenant with him as an everlasting covenant for his offspring after him."

(Genesis 17:15–19)

There's so much happening here that we need to unpack. Did you catch that Sarai was ninety years old, and her husband was one hundred? They believed there was no chance that having a baby was in the cards for them.

Sarai waited a long time to become a mother. We don't know when she began to long for a child, but we can assume that because she was married, and because bearing an heir for your husband was of utmost importance, she must have desired this.

Abram had said to the Lord in Genesis 15:2–4:

"O Lord GOD, what will you give me, for I continue childless, and the heir of my house is Eliezer of Damascus?" And Abram said, "Behold, you have given me no offspring, and a member of my household will be my heir." And behold, the word of the LORD came to him: "This man shall not be your heir; your very own son shall be your heir."

Abram was understandably concerned and probably downright confused. Here he was, in his eighties at the time of this scripture, and still without an heir. I'm certain he didn't think he would ever have children to call his own.

To complicate matters, Sarai made a decision that would alter the course of their history and tried to write the story they so desired. She asked Abram to go to her servant, Hagar, and let her have his baby. This would afford an heir to the house, and as a byproduct, Sarai would be a mom. As anyone could imagine, this plan created strife between the women:

> *And he went in to Hagar, and she conceived. And when she saw that she had conceived, she looked with contempt on her mistress. And Sarai said to Abram, "May the wrong done to me be on you! I gave my servant to your embrace, and when she saw that she had conceived, she looked on me with contempt. May the* Lord *judge between you and me!"*
>
> *(Genesis 16:4–5)*

The scripture shows us that Sarai projected her own contempt onto the woman she had given to her husband. I can't blame Sarai for feeling the way she did about Hagar after the fact. No matter how much she believed this was the answer to getting an heir, there was bound to be love lost between them. Sarai tried to "fix" this problem on her own. She wanted to create an heir to Abram's house and in doing so, she created a mess. I feel like the entirety of this story could be a reality show today with the highest of ratings. Our society loves a messy drama.

This is a lesson for those of us who don't like our times of waiting and attempt to make things happen ourselves, ahead of God's timing. Chaos came to Sarai when she tried to take matters into her own hands; she tried to create life without paying any mind to God's plan.

Sarai's desire to create human life through birth was unmet. However, I believe this desire to give life spans many areas of our lives. We long to give life to dreams, to ideas, to relationships of all kinds, to experiences, etc. There is bound to be something you wished existed in your life that has yet to be. These waiting periods can sometimes be the longest ones we will ever face.

I want to note a few things about Sarai's story that run parallel to our desires to give life today.

God's Purpose in Holding Onto New Life

The beauty of some of these stories in the Bible is the ability to see the ending written out so quickly after the beginning. In real life, and certainly for those who lived these stories in real time, this doesn't happen.

We see in Genesis 15 where Abram told God of his woe of not having children, and by Genesis 21, that desire was fulfilled. However, we know this was an excruciatingly long time for Sarai and Abram. (We can assume Sarai was feeling the same sadness as Abram.) And as Abram prayed to God, on multiple occasions God promised Abram a future he could not see and that, frankly, seemed unrealistic. For instance, in Genesis 15:4, God said that Abram's "very own son" would be his heir.

This story seems to wander off the beaten path when Abram has a child with his wife's servant. While he did have a son of his own with Hagar, that was not the son God was referring to when He promised his "very own son." God promised both Hagar and Abram, for different reasons, that their offspring would multiply beyond the ability to be numbered.

In Genesis 16:10, an angel of the Lord appeared to Hagar after her dispute with Sarai and said, "I will surely multiply your offspring so that they cannot be numbered for multitude." In Genesis 17:4, the Lord Himself said to Abram, "Behold my covenant is with you, and you shall be the father of a multitude of nations."

To a man who had waited his whole life to have children, I am sure this sounded preposterous. And to Hagar, who knew having a child with Abram would complicate her working and personal relationships with Sarai and Abram, this surely sounded outlandish.

I wish I could tell you, based on our current modern-day standards of marriage and correct relationship etiquette, exactly why God allowed this to happen the way He did. As I mentioned before, the messiness of this situation with Hagar can be attributed to Sarai's running ahead of the Lord's timing. However, one thing that we notice through Hagar's story is that even if this was not God's "first" plan, He can bring about blessings in the midst of chaos. He still had a plan to be worked out for the good of His kingdom *even though* these humans tried to plan things for themselves.

We know this to be true because of the promises the Bible tells us about these two children being born into this family. God said to Abram:

> *"I will make you exceedingly fruitful, and I will make you into nations, and kings shall come from you. And I will establish my covenant between me and you and your offspring after you throughout their generations for an everlasting covenant, to be God to you and to your offspring after you. And I will give to you and to your offspring after you the land of your sojournings, all the land of Canaan for an everlasting possession, and I will be their God."*
>
> *(Genesis 17:6–8)*

God's purpose in having Sarai and Abram wait to have their child was because generations and nations and kings to come would rely on the timing of Isaac's (their biological son's name given to him later in Genesis) birth.

Just as was for theirs, the Lord's destiny for your life is planned in advance and executed in His timing. Personally, as I am writing this right now, I long to have a fourth child. I can wish for it and even try for it while supposing that my timing is best because I know my life and my family's needs. However, if there is to be another child in our lives, God is timing his or her birth into this world because there is something purposeful in that baby's future. He has kingdom plans for my fourth child, and the birth timing is critical to that perfect plan.

This is true for my other children. They were born in the years they were because there is something in their lives the Lord has specifically planned for them to do, and they had to be born at a precise moment for the timing to line up.

This was true for Isaac, too. Sarai and Abram were the vehicles to deliver this timing; they were just unaware how long it would take.

This is also true for you. The time of your birth set in motion God's plan for your impact within His kingdom, but also for all the unborn desires of your heart. They each have a "birth point," and the timing is critical to the meeting of His will in your life and in the world around you.

Sometimes we think of our desires and ideas as small things, and we are the only ones who care about or will be impacted by them. But our God is bigger than that. My dream to be a writer was always my little dream in my tiny bedroom where I would fill journals with stories and ideas. I wanted to be "published" long before I ever actually was.

> God's purpose for your waiting is all about the right timing.

(A little sidenote: When I was in the fourth grade, that same teacher with the horses would supply me with paper bound into small booklets for me to write my own "books," and her son would illustrate them for me. This dream has been alive for a long time, and apparently that little farm had quite a large impact!)

But if I had been published before now, you wouldn't be the age you are right now and reading these words the Lord has inspired me to write. I wouldn't be the age I am with any of these life stories to tell. It's all in the timing. God's purpose for your waiting is all about the right timing.

Expecting God

I am sure Sarai and Abram expected that there would eventually be an end to their waiting. They were either going to have a child one day, or they would die one day, and with either option, their waiting would end.

However, if Sarai and Abram had only expected an end to their waiting, it wouldn't have allowed God to show up and prove His majesty and splendor. I don't think they knew to expect anything else, but waiting for *an end*, rather than waiting to experience God during that time, would have robbed them of the blessing a waiting season can produce.

You will have more waiting periods in life, and I am so hopeful that the next time you encounter one, you can position your heart to expect God to show up. If you simply start looking for Him within the waiting, it could change everything.

In this story, the Lord not only showed up in the promises He gave, but in the changing of their names. For those of you who have changed your name(s) at some point, marriage and adoption being the primary reasons, you understand what a big deal this is. You've been known as something your whole life, and then suddenly, you have a new name. You are someone different. Today, having been married for a decade, being called by my maiden name sounds so funny to me. And you wouldn't think that would be the case since I had that old name for twenty-six years, but that name just doesn't seem to fit who I am anymore.

Not everyone decides to change their name when they get married. Whether you change your name or not, you step into a new role as a spouse when you make the decision to get married. One of the representations of this can be changing your name. For me personally, my new name is a symbol of stepping into a new place that God had created for me as a wife.

I first became a mom through adoption. Our son had four names given to him by his birth mother, and we decided to change two of those names when we adopted him. He came home to us when he was four years old, and if you were to ask him today what his old last name was, he would look at you funny. To him, he has always been a Ribble. You see, when he stepped into the future the Lord had for him as a beloved son, he needed a new name.

For Sarai and Abram to step into the future He had for them, they needed new names. I have continued to speak about Sarai and Abram as exactly that—Sarai and Abram. However, we mainly know them as Sarah and Abraham. I used *Sarai* so much in previous paragraphs to drive home the point that for the majority of her life, that was how she was known. The same goes for Abraham, he was known as Abram until he was ninety-nine years old. For us, that would have been our whole lives.

God proved He was there with Sarai and Abram when He changed their names. In Genesis 17:4–5, He said,

"Behold, my covenant is with you, and you shall be the father of a multitude of nations. No longer shall your name be called Abram, but your name shall be Abraham, for I have made you the father of a multitude of nations."

God stated His promise and then changed Abram's name to Abraham. The change between these names isn't all that much—two letters, in fact—and the names sound very similar. Abram's name had always meant "exalted father," but the change made in his name would add a root word that meant "multitude." Thus, the meaning of Abraham meant "father of a multitude."[4]

Anyone can change their name. You can choose any name you want and decide to be known by that, but only God can take a name, change its meaning, and *fulfill the meaning of your name*. Hear this again: *Only God can fulfill the meaning of your name*. Only He can make a meaning come to life.

> Only God can fulfill the meaning of your name. Only He can make a meaning come to life.

Just as God did this with Abram (now known as Abraham), He did this for Sarai. God told Abraham:

"As for Sarai your wife, you shall not call her name Sarai, but Sarah shall be her name. I will bless her, and moreover, I will give you a son by her. I will bless her, and she shall become nations; kings of peoples shall come from her."

(Genesis 17:15–16)

Once again, the Lord came in and fulfilled His promises with the action of changing the meaning of Sarai's name. Just as with Abram, He didn't change the name to a completely different name; He made a tweak that expanded the meaning of Abram's name. Sarai's name had meant "princess" or "princely." By deciding that people should refer to her as Sarah, which was simply just a different way to say Sarai (based on dialect), it opened up the meaning to "chieftainess" or "commander" or "captain."[5] Though her name still meant "princess," the meaning blossomed to mean so much more.

Sarah was going to be the mother of nations to come, of kings to come. What profound truth for a woman who had waited ninety years to give life to a single baby!

Their names needed to change so that the meaning of their names matched the destiny God had created for them. (If this doesn't make you want to run a million laps in excitement, I'm not sure much else will. This is a powerful truth for all of us to own.)

Neither Abraham nor Sarah could see the end in sight. They had lived longer than many of us live today without seeing their hearts' desires to be parents come to fruition. It was difficult for them to *expect God in the waiting* rather than *expect an end to their waiting*. But one of the ways the Lord showed up for them in the waiting was by changing their names. He took their names, tweaked their meanings, then promised that these symbolized their destinies.

Think about your own life. Do you know the meaning of your name? Even if the meaning of your name isn't something profound, you can ask God to give meaning to your name. The beautiful thing is, if you don't know what His meaning for you is, He already has one. Ask Him to reveal it to you and to show you in this waiting period of life just what fulfillment of promise He has for you.

This waiting is not wasted. Expect God, and then waiting for the end will not be so agonizing.

God Provides Life

Seeing the life infused into Abraham and Sarah's story is easy, as an actual human life resulted from their waiting season. However, the life given in their waiting season can parallel the *life* that is given to our waiting seasons . . . if we are willing to see it, willing to shift our definition of life away from *birth* and to *creation, ideas,* or *dreams.*

First, let's see what the Lord did for them. After He told Abraham that Sarah would give birth to his son, Abraham laughed:

> *Then Abraham fell on his face and laughed and said to himself, "Shall a child be born to a man who is a hundred years old? Shall Sarah, who is ninety years old, bear a child?"*
>
> *(Genesis 17:17)*

Then in the next chapter, Sarah also found the news amusing:

> *So Sarah laughed to herself, saying, "After I am worn out, and my lord is old, shall I have pleasure?"*
>
> *(Genesis 18:12)*

The Hebrew word translated for when Abraham laughed to himself means "he said this in his heart." These weren't audible words; he was pondering how surprising God's promise was. It made him laugh inside. I imagine his and Sarah's "laughter" was both disbelief and elation wrapped up in one. I find it so appropriate that He decided their son's name would be Isaac, which means "laughter." What a joyful name for a little boy who would be the heir to many, many nations and many, many thrones!

Abraham and Sarah were given abundant life after such a long waiting period. *Abundant* means something that exists in large quantities, and, boy, did God give to them in abundance! He gave them a son who would multiply into nations and kingdoms. What exquisite opulence for two people who felt that the Lord had forgotten them within a lifelong waiting season!

What kind of abundant life are you seeking? This might be actual life as you have been trying to become a parent, or it could be life you want infused back into a relationship, or life you want to see in an idea or a dream you've had.

We all look for and long for dreams to become reality. Maybe the career you've dreamed of having has felt so far out of reach, but you long to give "life" to that dream one day. You could have also dreamed of having a particular car or a certain house, and you look forward to making those dreams become reality one day.

Did you know God longs for you to have the desires of your heart? Not only does He long for you to have the life you dream of having, most often the reality He has for you is bigger and better than your dreams.

Abraham and Sarah are the perfect example of this concept. They longed to have one baby, but God desired to have generations upon generations come from them.

No dream is too big for God. And no matter how long you wait for your dreams to take flight, He desires to give you abundant life at the end of your waiting season. If you don't believe me, just look at His words to Abraham in Genesis 18:13–14: "Why did Sarah laugh and say 'Shall I indeed bear a child, now that I am old?' Is anything too hard for the LORD?"

> No dream is too big for God.

Is anything too hard for the Lord? This rhetorical question is met with a resounding NO. There is *nothing* God cannot do, including allowing a ninety-year-old woman to have a baby. Again, there is nothing your God cannot do. Nothing. Remember this, friend.

THREE

Waiting FOR LOVE

Wherever you are, whenever it's right
You'll come out of nowhere and into my life
—*Michael Bublé, "Haven't Met You Yet"*[6]

How long would you wait to find your true love? How long would you tarry in an unrequited state? We all long to be with the one the Lord has made for us. For most of us, being with the person who completes us is a desire we want to fulfill more than anything else. The story of Jacob is one that is quite heartbreaking. Jacob waited and worked for the one his heart loved only to be met with an unbelievable amount of time without her.

Some of you are in the season of waiting on your forever mate. However, if you aren't currently in a season of waiting on your love, because you have already found that person, my hope is that God shows up through Jacob's story and will help you reaffirm, reclaim, and/or reconnect with the love He has given you.

Maybe this is not a love with another human; maybe this is the love you have for God. Whomever He is laying on your heart—lean in and listen, friend. This waiting period is heavy.

Here we meet Jacob, and if you've read the chapters in Genesis preceding this, you are all too familiar with his heritage of waiting: Jacob was the son of Isaac (yep, *that* Isaac, the son born to Sarah and Abraham after many years of waiting). Genesis 28 shows us Isaac sending his son Jacob off to go live in Paddan-aram. Isaac said to Jacob in verses 3–4:

> *"God Almighty bless you and make you fruitful and multiply you, that you may become a company of peoples. May he give the blessing of Abraham to you and to your offspring with you, that you may take possession of the land of your sojournings that God gave to Abraham!"*

Notice how Isaac admonished God to give to Jacob the blessing of Abraham. What is fascinating is we read in the previous chapter how God promised *all* of this blessing to Abraham. He promised Abraham that he would be the father of many nations, that he would prosper in the land that God had set apart for him. This meant *all* of Abraham's offspring would inherit this gift. However, they were still asking God for the promise He had already made to them through Abraham. They were still doing the work to hope and pray for the blessings that He had *already* promised.

Think about yourself for a moment. Have you ever been in a season in which you were waiting on something from God, and He made it known what He had in store for you, yet you continued to pray and ask because you couldn't *see* His promise yet with your eyes? And maybe I should back up a little bit, because it's often very difficult to know when He is speaking to you to know if He has promised you something.

I have found the easiest ways to know when the Lord is speaking to you, is to know what His voice sounds like. I get it, this sounds weird. Let me explain.

I know my husband's voice because I have memorized not only what it sounds like, but also the way in which he says things. Someone could be an impeccable impersonator and mimic his voice to me, but unless they phrased things exactly how he would say them, I would know it wasn't him. Basically, I know his voice because I know what *is not* his voice. The same can be said of God's voice. You have to learn what His voice *is not.* Over time, I have learned that His voice does not make me feel less than, does not cause me anxiety, and does not cause me to fear. His voice will also not lead me to destruction or wrath. When I feel emotions such as these, I know they are not from God.

> Over time, I have learned that His voice does not make me feel less than, does not cause me anxiety, and does not cause me to fear.

When I have asked Him for something in my life, I don't get immediate answers . . . nor do I expect to. But over time, as I think about the things I am wanting in my life, if my emotions around that subject are filled with love and hope and peace, I know He is speaking blessing over this. If I think upon something and it gives me anxiety or fear or makes me feel terrible about myself, I know that He is not causing these emotions, and I must be setting my heart in the wrong direction.

2 Timothy 1:7 says, "for God gave us a spirit not of fear but of power and love and self-control." To know His voice is to know what His voice *is not.*

Abraham believed the promise God made to him in his heart (mainly because he knew the voice of the Lord over his long relationship with Him), but he truly knew the truth of God's promise when he saw Isaac's face. Here we are again, one generation later, and Isaac continued to pray for what had already been promised to him; and he taught Jacob to do the same.

I am sure we all do this time and time again, and I view it in two ways: with frustration that we continue to ask God for what He has already promised because we don't currently have what is coming to us. But I also view this as a sweet reminder that *our relationship with the Lord does not end when He gives what He promises. The continual longings in our souls and hearts propel us to relationship with Him.* I find that quite beautiful. Our desires and wants help continue communion with the Lord.

Seldom do our promises start with us. And seldom are our waiting periods the first of their kind. Nothing is new under the sun. Yours is a generation marked by repeated waiting periods from those before you and repeated promises of what God would do for them.

So Jacob set out on his journey, and just as his grandfather before him, he longed to be a father one day. To accomplish that, he would have to find love. Along Jacob's journey to his new home, he stopped to rest and while he rested, God appeared to him in a dream:

And he dreamed, and behold, there was a ladder set up on the earth, and the top of it reached to heaven. And behold, the angels of God were ascending and descending on it! And behold, the LORD stood above it and said, "I am the LORD, the God of Abraham your father and the God of Isaac. The land on which you lie I will give to you and to your offspring. Your offspring shall be like the dust of the earth, and you shall spread abroad to the west and to the east and to the north and to the south, and in you and your offspring shall all the families of the earth be blessed. Behold, I am with you and will keep you wherever you go, and will bring you back to this land. For I will not leave you until I have done what I have promised you." Then Jacob awoke from his sleep and said, "Surely the LORD is in this place, and I did not know it." And he was afraid and said, "How awesome is this place! This is none other than the house of God, and this is the gate of heaven."

(Genesis 28:12–17)

There is God again, repeating the promise of Abraham because Jacob wasn't alive to hear it then, but now he is, as an inheritor of the *original* promise. The story goes on to say that Jacob found the land to which his father had sent him. He was supposed to go find his mother's brother (Laban) and his family. Isaac felt sure that Jacob should go live among those people and serve there. Jacob arrived and saw Rachel, the daughter of Laban, and he was love struck.

Laban was elated that Jacob was there and wanted Jacob to work for him, but since they were family, he wanted to pay him appropriately. They made a deal in Genesis 29:15–20:

"Because you are my kinsman, should you therefore serve me for nothing? Tell me, what shall your wages be?" Now Laban had two daughters. The name of the older was Leah, and the name of the younger was Rachel. Leah's eyes were weak, but Rachel was beautiful in form and appearance. Jacob loved Rachel. And he said, "I will serve you seven years for your younger daughter Rachel." Laban said, "It is better that I give her to you than that I should give her to any other man; stay with me." So Jacob served seven years for Rachel, and they seemed to him but a few days because of the love he had for her.

(Sidenote: Let's first just put it on the table that this whole thing is strange. We aren't going to get into the complicated family relations. That's another book. Moving on.)

How sweet and Hallmark-ish that the Bible says that Jacob's seven years only seemed like a few days because of the love he had for Rachel. Insert all the heart eyes and Jim and Pam googly-eyed GIFs here (if you are unsure of the reference, please look up and binge *The Office*). Jacob's story was a messy one. If you continue reading in Genesis, you will find a lot of heartache and waiting periods for both him and Rachel (and the other wives he had and his children with them).

There are two things to note here about Jacob's initial waiting to marry Rachel; let's look at those now.

God's Purpose in Preparing for Love

For God to fulfill the promises he made to Abraham, there had to be many children to come. It takes *a lot* of children to populate nations. And while it's easy for us to see that on this side of the story, Jacob and Rachel had a difficult time seeing the promises that He had given as a part of their active lives.

God was going to fulfill His promise to Abraham through Jacob as well, but He would do it in *His* timing, not Jacob's. Notice in Genesis 29:21 Jacob said to Laban, "Give me my wife that I may go in to her, for my time is completed." Laban then prepared a celebratory feast. At the end of the night, however, Laban tricked Jacob by giving Leah (his oldest daughter) to him, as it was customary of the time for the oldest daughter to be married first. And then Laban tricked Jacob into working *another* seven years for the gift of Rachel.

Jacob was willing to wait the first seven years for the love of his life, but he never considered if the Lord was ready *or* if Rachel was ready. It's easy to read this story and feel so incredibly sorry for Jacob; and I do, believe me. However, two sets of seven years was Laban's—*not* God's—timing. Sometimes our waiting period is not just for God to ready us, but for Him to ready those around us.

One of my dearest friends in all the world met her husband when she was thirty years old. She once told me, "I'm thankful for the time I had as I was single just because the Lord used that time in my life to prepare me for [my husband] and just to give me time to myself to be able to fully serve the Lord and concentrate on that."

Her personal timing of meeting the man she wanted to marry had come and gone before she ever met her future husband. But as she looks back on the timing, God had a lot for her to do in those years that she may not have accomplished had she gotten married sooner.

This was true for Jacob, as well. Though the Bible doesn't say specifically what Jacob did in those seven years, we know because of what is written later how much of an impact he had on Laban and the people of Paddan-aram. In Genesis 31, Jacob talked about all he did for Laban during the twenty years he served him (he served six additional years after marrying Rachel to earn livestock). Laban and all of his family prospered because of Jacob's work and devotion to his calling to be there with him. There was so much growth and life that happened in Jacob's waiting period. The same happened for my friend. She was able to accomplish a lot for God in her time of waiting.

God's purpose for your waiting periods may simply be to prepare your life, and someone else's life, so that at the exact right moment in time, you collide when you should. That is definitely my story with my husband. We are five years apart, which is not a lot, but when you meet can depend on what time of life you are in. I often joke with him about me being in middle school when he was starting college. (When he talks about a band he listened to back in the day, I act like I don't know if he's talking about a movie or a person, because I was "just a child then." Ha!)

When I was twenty-two, I was so ready to meet the man I would marry. I was finishing college, and every gal around me was wedding planning or close to it. But when I was twenty-two, my future husband was twenty-seven and had long been working in his career; college was a distant memory for him. At twenty-two, I was ready to have already known him and be starting my life with him. But I hadn't even met him yet. I wouldn't meet him until I was twenty-four, and I wouldn't start my forever with him until two years later.

Right now, that four-year difference seems like a couple seconds, but when I was twenty-two—sitting in my car crying about an unknown future and in a failing relationship—those dreams of getting married seemed so far away. And that wonderful thing called hindsight shows me now that when I longed to know my husband, he wasn't ready to know me yet. Why? Because he had already made the decision to settle down with someone else. Meeting me at twenty-two would have done no good. He wasn't even looking.

> The purpose of this waiting period is often for preparation of two hearts to meet when the timing is right.

Our meet-cute had to happen at the exact right time for *both* of our hearts—when I was further along in my life and when he was unattached. The purpose of this waiting period is often for preparation of two hearts to meet when the timing is right. Within that purpose are things the Lord is accomplishing in your waiting.

Expecting God

As I mentioned, when I was twenty-two, I truly thought I was meant to marry a guy who wasn't right for me (the guy I was crying over in my car that day). I had spent three years of my life with him, and I was dreaming of the life we could build together. I prayed for our future, all the while still praying for characteristics I longed to be true of the man I would one day marry. I prayed for someone to be loyal, someone to be consistent in their words and deeds, someone to love me at every phase of my life and body weight, someone who shared my love for God and the passions I felt He was laying on my life, and someone who would be proud of who I was. Unfortunately, I was praying for someone entirely different than the guy I was dating. What a concept. The whole time I was focusing my prayers in the direction of this particular person, it turned out that he was not, in fact, the person those prayers were truly about.

Through this, I learned that our prayers are often preparing us for a destiny our dreams do not have the ability to create. I could have dreamed every waking moment for my future husband and still not have been able to imagine exactly how perfect he would be for me.

One of the strongest lessons I learned through that time of longing and prayer was how much the Lord wanted my relationship with Him to supersede all the other relationships I had. My prayers began to slowly shift from focusing so much on an earthly relationship to focusing on the relationship I had with my heavenly Father. If I had that relationship right, the others would fall into place.

Our waiting periods are not specifically meant for us to sit and do nothing while our promises come through. Sometimes that waiting period is for God to rekindle (or start) His relationship with us, and this takes commitment on our part. Sometimes waiting for love is not for a human love here on earth, but for a beginning or a reconnection with the One who loves you most, Jesus.

For my friend, God was able not only to do a lot through her time of singleness, but He was able to give her vision for the future and direction for her plans, and He sustained her with His love for her. You see, He was always her first love, and His presence while she awaited her second love was paramount to her success in navigating the length of time He would have her waiting.

This can be said of Jacob. The Lord was cultivating the ground for the generations to come (that had been promised to his grandfather, Abraham), which would take a lot of time. He used this time to serve people through Jacob's willing hands. Then God continued to cultivate a personal relationship with Jacob so that he would be able to navigate all God had planned for him. As I previously mentioned, Jacob was a man who would have a lot of hard things to walk through, and this was just the beginning. God knew Jacob would need a firm foundation in his relationship with Him, and this time of waiting was meant to plant the seeds of love and care that Jacob would need to harvest later.

You will need a firm spiritual foundation with God to help steady your marriage when it assuredly comes upon trying times. There is no "*if* you have difficult times," but "*when* you have difficult times" in marriage. Marriage is the coming together of two very different people with individual personalities, wants, and needs, while also living in as much harmony as possible. While this seems like a tough situation to be in, this is a recipe that can lead to a ton of happiness, but a lot of work goes into maintaining that happiness.

I stood next to that friend I keep talking about on her wedding day and in her vows I heard her say these words to her husband, "You're not the man of my dreams . . .

you are the man of my prayers." Her husband had not shown up in her life when she'd planned, and when he did show up, he did not look at all like she had imagined. He was not the man she had dreamed of, but he was most certainly the man she had prayed for. Oftentimes, what we pray for doesn't look like what we dream about and for good reason.

Jacob saw Rachel and thought it would be so simple to dream of having just her for all of eternity. But the Lord knew the prayers Jacob prayed back in Genesis 28 would be better for him if he acquired what he prayed for then and not what he dreamed of now.

> Oftentimes, what we pray for doesn't look like what we dream about and for good reason.

Then Jacob made a vow, saying, "If God will be with me and will keep me in this way that I go, and will give me bread to eat and clothing to wear, so that I come again to my father's house in peace, then the LORD shall be my God, and this stone, which I have set up for a pillar, shall be God's house. And of all that you give me I will give a full tenth to you."

(Genesis 28:20–22)

Jacob prayed for the blessings God would give if he obeyed His commands to "go." He couldn't be prepared for all that would follow, but his obedience would bring a lot of good and a lot of trying things. What he dreamed of was so simple and less complex than what God had in store for him. A quiet life with only Rachel would not have resulted in the kingdoms and generations Abraham was promised. Jacob needed what he prayed for, not what he dreamed of.

Think about how much praying you do in the waiting. All of those moments spent praying are connecting you with your heavenly Father. You may be dreaming of having conversations with your future spouse, but just think about all the conversations you get to have with the Lord when you are praying for your heart's desires and His will to happen in your life. You are cultivating the deepest relationship with the One who loves you most.

I don't know about you, but I am really glad my promises in life aren't left up to *my* dreams and *my* plans. God always knows better, and I want what *He* has for me. I don't want to settle for less than His best.

As my friend said, "I'm so glad the Lord didn't go off of my list, because He knew so much better than I did."

Trust the process, friend. Trust that this waiting season is preparing you, and preparing the one for you, in ways you would never be able to know. When the timing is right, you will be propelled forward to a new horizon you could never have dreamed possible. And you will be able to say, just as Jacob did in Genesis 28:17 when God showed him his promises, "How awesome is this place! This is none other than the house of God, and this is the gate of heaven."

Wait for the "gate of heaven" feeling. You will never be disappointed.

FOUR

Waiting FOR FORGIVENESS

I will restore to you the years
that the swarming locust has eaten.

—Joel 2:25

You know who they are. As soon as you read the title
of this chapter, you could see their faces. You could
hear the last words they said to you. You are either waiting
to receive their forgiveness, lingering on final words that
left a wake in your relationship, or maybe even waiting for
them to forgive you.

Unfortunately, close relationships are often torn apart
by words, time, and deeds. I've witnessed how hurtful
words within my own blood family have severed relationships for years. I've attended funerals where people

had to say their apologies too late. Even if you haven't seen this firsthand, you likely know where the earthquakes happened in your family that created fault lines for generations.

For some of you, forgiveness is an *end* you look forward to reaching. For some of you reading this, forgiveness isn't on the horizon at all. And for others, you no longer even consider forgiveness; that ship has sailed. You know that age-old saying of "forgive and forget," right? Well, if we are honest with ourselves, we can often work toward forgiveness, but seldom can we forget.

This was the case for Joseph in the Bible. He was no stranger to this concept. In fact, he waited decades before he would ever be able to offer forgiveness to the people he held most dear: his father and brothers.

Joseph was the son of Jacob and Rachel, whom you read about in the last chapter. Jacob and Leah (his first wife, Rachel's sister) had many children, and Jacob also had children with both his wives' servants. But Rachel herself, it seemed, was barren. But as we know, God has a way of making these things happen, and in her old age, she was blessed with Joseph, who became Jacob's favorite son at his birth. You see the Lord's promises to Abraham continuing to multiply here in Joseph's story, but not without a lot of heartache to go around.

Genesis 37 recounts his story for us. In verse 3, we discover that because of his being favored by their father, Joseph's brothers hated him. So much so that they made a plan to sell him away and lie to their father about what happened to him. The rest of the chapter details their plot, in which they kidnapped him, sold him to traders, and then made it seem that he had been killed.

What could be God's purpose in this? I am sure Joseph felt a million things. If his own family did not love him enough to let him even be a part of them, where in the world would he be accepted?

Joseph would go on to be sold in Egypt to Potiphar, who was an officer of the pharaoh. There, Joseph became an incredibly successful man, managing everything Potiphar owned, and then one day he became so highly favored that he was promoted to be higher than anyone in Egypt except Pharaoh himself.

Genesis 41:40–44 gives us the exchange between Pharaoh and Joseph that altered the course of his entire life and that of history. Pharaoh said to him,

"You shall be over my house, and all my people shall order themselves as you command. Only as regards the throne will I be greater than you." And Pharaoh said to Joseph, "See, I have set you over all the land

of Egypt." Then Pharaoh took his signet ring from his hand and put it on Joseph's hand, and clothed him in garments of fine linen and put a gold chain about his neck. And he made him ride in his second chariot. And they called out before him, "Bow the knee!" Thus he set him over all the land of Egypt. Moreover, Pharaoh said to Joseph, "I am Pharaoh, and without your consent no one shall lift up hand or foot in all the land of Egypt."

Can you imagine? Having been thrown away by your family (literally, in a pit by your own brothers) and just a few decades later risen to the highest spot in all the land of Egypt? There's no way for us to fathom the surrealness of that moment. What elation Joseph must have felt, yet at the same time, what heartache must have resounded through him to know his father could not see this moment. Would he ever see his brothers again? Would he ever hug his father again? Would all this success fill the void from not having his family? From the accounts we have, it seems that Joseph was separated from his family for about twenty-two years. That is such a long time to be separated from the ones you love.

You may be separated by hours or days or decades from the one(s) you love and care for. You may have hurled words you didn't mean; they may have done unfor-givable deeds, or you both could be at the ends of a wrong thrust upon you by someone else. Whatever the case is, *Joseph's story screams to us that nothing is ever too far gone from the Lord's mending hands.* In fact, there is so much He is doing in you and in those around you during this waiting time.

Journey with me, friend. Let's find the Lord within this hurtful suspension of time.

God's Purpose in Pruning Relationships

All throughout the Bible, you see God preparing a place or preparing people for something He is about to do. Joseph's story is riddled with prepara-tion. The brothers may have thought they were in control when they sold Joseph away, but little did they know, the Lord was using their evil for His good. Situations can hap-pen, words can be said, hurt-ful actions can be taken, and yet He will use them to prepare a place for reconciliation to grow. Sometimes the hurt and pain caused by the rip

> Sometimes the hurt and pain caused by the rip in a relationship is the pruning the ground needs to plant new seeds again.

in a relationship is the pruning the ground needs to plant new seeds again.

Think about the hardening of hearts that can happen from past hurts. Some of the most hurtful conversations I have had or been privy to have taken place within the walls of a church. I grew up in a pastor's home, and unfortunately, the church politics and preferences you see behind the curtain are often quite ugly. My dad was also the child of a pastor, and throughout my life, he would recount this story of witnessing some men in his father's church bash my grandfather verbally in a very public manner. This situation caused my dad to turn away from the church for a long time. But, as God's sense of humor goes sometimes, He led my dad into the same life.

There have been two instances when my brother and I watched as people we had been taught to trust within our church walls came after our dad in very public and very malicious ways. No matter who did what and to whom, seeing your father verbally abused and ripped apart by people who claim to be followers of Jesus is a lifelong, scarring incident. As I mentioned in a previous chapter, you know the voice of the Lord mainly by knowing what His voice is not. And I can tell you with absolute certainty, when the words spoken by these people were hurled in my dad's direction, they did not sound like Jesus at all.

Words and deeds like this have caused a chasm in my heart and soul that has still not healed years later. You see, I have worked with God privately to forgive these people for what they did, but I will never be able to forget their actions. And in my situation, these individuals are not people who should ever be in my life again because of the toxic nature of their actions.

We can forgive people and harbor no ill will toward them and still move on in life without them. In my case, these were verbally abusive people who sought to hurt our family. For some of you, the abuse may be physical or mental. And if the relationships from *my* past are not meant to be mended, certainly the Lord can help you purge an abuser from your life and also lead you to forgive them. There is toxicity that can live in a relationship, leaving it truly unmendable. So, keep in mind, there are times God is pruning, and He doesn't mean for reconciliation to grow.

Joseph's story points us to a different type of forgiveness: the forgiveness of those relationships the Lord longs to see reprised. The child who left home when they could no longer see eye to eye with family, the friend who couldn't understand your decisions in life, the spouse meant for you but there were hurtful actions prying you apart, etc. The ground in which these relationships originally bloomed became full of weeds and needed tending. If you think of the waiting period of forgiveness as a time of pruning to plant new seeds, it's easy to see how this takes time. For the purpose of this chapter, let's talk about wheat.

You see, Joseph was overseeing Egypt when a great famine was approaching. His father and brothers were suffering greatly, and this is what propelled Joseph's father to send his brothers to Egypt to buy food—Egypt was plentiful in provisions.

When Jacob learned that there was grain for sale in Egypt, he said to his sons, "Why do you look at one another?" And he said, "Behold, I have heard that there is grain for sale in Egypt. Go down and buy grain for us there, that we may live and not die."

(Genesis 42:1–2)

Egypt was known for selling many things, but grain, or wheat, was one of the most plentiful. Do you know how long it takes to grow wheat? About seven or eight months. You plant and you wait more than half a year for it to reach maturity.

Seven or eight months. Joseph lived in Egypt through twenty-two wheat seasons. If you do the math, that's at least 154 months Joseph watched the crops grow and fielded the requests of people needing food. He was the gatekeeper of the grains—at least by the time his brothers came along needing some. Do you ever wonder how many times he looked in the eyes of the men coming for grain and wondered if they were his family?

It takes time to grow the grain that will feed your body and soul. You can't just plant it and *will* it to come up immediately. It doesn't work that way. I've watched my husband dethatch and seed our yard and then look at the ground every day for evidence of his work. But all the looking in the world will not make that seed grow; you have to wait until the time is right to see the buds begin to show through.

Maybe God has allowed a rift to happen in your life because He needs to re-seed the ground for more grain to sustain you and your loved ones for the future. Maybe there is an abundance of harvest prepared for you, but He has to ready the ground for that to happen. This would most certainly be the story of Joseph. God had a lot of blessing to come his way—and ultimately his family's way—but had the rift not happened, where would that harvest have been?

Wouldn't you rather this relationship reap a harvest when the time of forgiveness is right? Walk the path of waiting for the Lord to do work within you and within those around you.

God Preserves Life

I talked earlier in this book about how I believe God uses our times of waiting to preserve us. I believe He sometimes suspends us in time in order to preserve, to keep, something within us that He loves.

Joseph mentioned this exact concept when he finally spoke to his brothers:

*So Joseph said to his brothers, "Come near to me, please." And they came near. And he said, "I am your brother, Joseph, whom you sold into Egypt. And now do not be distressed or angry with yourselves because you sold me here, for **God sent me before you to preserve life**. For the famine has been in the land these two years, and there are yet five years in which there will be neither plowing nor harvest. And **God sent me before you to preserve for you a remnant on earth**, and to keep alive for you many survivors. So, it was not you who sent me here, but God.*

He has made me a father to Pharaoh, and lord of all his house and ruler over all the land of Egypt. Hurry and go up to my father and say to him, 'Thus says your son Joseph, God has made me lord of all Egypt. Come down to me; do not tarry. You shall dwell in the land of Goshen, and you shall be near me, you and your children and your children's children, and your flocks, your herds, and all that you have. There I will provide for you, for there are yet five years of famine to come, so that you and your household, and all that you have, do not come to poverty."

(Genesis 45:4–11, emphasis added)

Notice two things: One, Joseph said, "It was not you who sent me here, but God" (verse 8). He made it clear that even though his brothers did something meant for harm, God had a plan all along that was meant for good. Your waiting period is not meant to tear you down and leave you destitute. You may think and feel that at times, but that is not the case. This waiting period is meant for good. It is meant to preserve you.

Which brings us to Joseph's next statement, "For God sent me before you to preserve life." Joseph talked about the famine that had been in the land, which was what had driven his brothers to Egypt in the first place. Joseph knew the famine wasn't going to end soon. Egypt had positioned itself well during the famine because they were able to store grain from all the previous years when the harvest had been plentiful. Thus, even though the famine was hitting Egypt, too, people were coming to them from all around to buy grain because their towns did not have that same luxury.

Joseph believed God had sent him to Egypt to preserve his family, to keep them. God knew twenty-two years in advance that the famine was coming, and while He had a plan for everyone touched by it, our Bible gives us one story about Jacob and his sons and how He specifically took care of them. He sent Joseph ahead, made him lord of the land, and gave him the power to feed his family in the largest famine they would ever see.

If the Lord was so specific in His plan for Joseph and his family, you can bet He was taking care of those around Joseph just as well. He was preserving food specifically to feed Joseph's father and brothers for years to come. And this would be the tool needed to bring them together in order for reconciliation to begin.

Food isn't the only thing that sometimes needs preserving. Take my friend Wes, whose marriage ended harshly many years ago. He and his former wife share four grown children together, and they have been caught up in the middle of their parents' issues. Sides have been taken, and unfortunately for Wes, most often the children have sided with their mother.

It doesn't really matter who is right or wrong; what is most prominent now is a father in his old age who longs for a relationship with his children. I once overheard a friend ask Wes, "So what do you do to try and repair the relationships?" He responded, "I just show up and keep loving them. Be there if they need something. Answer the phone if they decide to call. Just keep loving them."

Wes wouldn't be able to put this into words because the scars run so very deep, but you see what he's doing, right? He keeps storing up the love he has for the day they come to him in need of it. He gives love if they come for it now, but he stores the multitudes for when the famine is so great, they need it all.

> We all need some sort of nourishment in the waiting.

Food might not be the thing you need right now. Maybe your need is similar to Wes's, and you need love reciprocated through trust. But food nourishes, just as love does, and *we all need some sort of nourishment in the waiting*. Maybe the Lord has suspended you in this time so He can gather nourishment to shower on you later.

It's all about the timing, friend. You must meet God's will when it is ready to rain down on you. You don't want to be too early, or even too late; you could starve. Rest in the waiting.

FIVE

Waiting IN THE WILDERNESS

The wilderness is a place of preparation, not permanence.

—*Lisa Appelo, blogger and encourager*[7]

Think about the time your life felt most desert-like. Maybe you felt like you were wandering without purpose with no landmarks to guide your way or lights to show you where you were. Perhaps you felt like you were thirsting to death, and there was no refreshment in sight. Maybe everything just seemed so bleak, and as far as you looked, all you could see was a never-ending trail of the same.

I remember feeling this way after college. I had plenty of ambition and drive, but I also felt so lost and wasn't sure which way to go. I made plans for grad school that fell through at the last minute. I ended up landing a job that was perfect for me, but I knew in my heart I wasn't supposed to be there forever. My life felt fraught with uncertainty. The previous four years in college, I pretty much knew what would happen from year to year. But after college, for the first time in my life, I couldn't see the road in front of me, and I was downright frightened. I knew the Lord was there, because I was a woman of faith even then, but without being able to trace His hand on a map, I was beginning to wonder if He had left me alone. I was moving from one period of my life to the next, and this transition would feel long and lonesome in so many ways.

I imagine Moses felt some of these same emotions as he was tasked with leading God's people out of Egypt, where they had been slaves, to freedom. However, this freedom came at a cost. They had been living through hard times for a long time at the hand of the pharaoh. But even in attempting to leave, what lay before them were massive amounts of unpredictability.

We read the story of the exodus in which Moses led the Israelites across dry land in the middle of the Red Sea, all while Pharaoh's army pursued them. When we reach the end of the story, we'd like to think, *Whew! It's over!* and close the book on what was a wild adventure. But that is only the intermission: The people of Israel were waiting for freedom, and they had so much work to do in order to achieve it.

It's easy to define this time in history by the Red Sea moment. No doubt, that moment shows us a massive thing about how God shows up for His people. Many times, when people think of Moses, they think of him parting the Red Sea, and thus the rest of his time in the wilderness is overlooked. However, that moment was bookended by two waiting periods that drug His people through thick uncertainty.

You've probably experienced wilderness like this—a desolate time in which the Lord moved you from one place to another, leaving you to internally (and maybe externally) question His leading. Maybe He moved you physically from one place to the next, and you were scared. Maybe He moved you from one job to another, and while you were excited to move on, the unknown was frightening. Or maybe He moved you from one job to another but the change was unwelcomed. Maybe He moved you on from a relationship that had run its course, and leaving familiarity

> When the Lord is moving you into the wilderness for a period of time unknown to you, He has plans in the desert.

seemed daunting. Maybe God is currently moving you physically, emotionally, and mentally to a new phase in life, and you cannot see what is on the other side at all.

I'm here to tell you that *when the Lord is moving you into the wilderness for a period of time unknown to you, He has plans in the desert.* Even though the wilderness definitely seems like an unwelcoming place, I would rather be there, in the wilderness, if I knew God was going to show up than in a place without Him.

It may sound cheesy, but as the American Christian recording artist Steven Curtis Chapman sings in "The Great Adventure," let's "follow our leader into the glorious unknown!"[8]

Believe it or not, there can be a lot of good to come from the great unknown, and the Israelites certainly learned this the hard way.

God's Purpose in Wandering

The Israelites voiced their concerns to Moses when he was instructing them to leave Egypt. The end of their statement in Exodus 14:12 says, "For it would have been better for us to serve the Egyptians than to die in the wilderness." They truly believed, in those hard moments of wandering, that they would have been better off staying as slaves to Pharaoh than making the attempted journey to freedom. For them, they couldn't see a successful end in sight, so they couldn't believe the waiting period would lead to victory.

We are the same as the Israelites. Sometimes we ask to stay in the comfort of what we know, even if it hurts, because the unknown is scary. Think about a time when God nudged you to move on, when He opened the door and said, "Walk." If you hesitated for even a moment, or for days and weeks, think about the feelings you laid in when He was paving a way forward. Was it worth the hesitation? Should you have listened sooner?

Almost every time I have encountered a moment like this in my life, when I get to the other side I say, "I wish I had done this sooner." Right? Haven't you felt that way?

My family moved a lot when I was a child. To date, I have personally moved seventeen times. My dad's job at the time laid the foundation of this constant uprooting. When I was very young, he managed retail stores around the country, which meant his role was to open stores and get them running well or to close a store and move it elsewhere. This meant we were moving every six months.

When I was in early elementary school, my dad went into full-time ministry and became a pastor. While I lived at home, he pastored four different churches in two states. I distinctly remember that when Dad felt the Lord asking him to move on, he exuded a steadiness that I studied thoroughly. I'm sure in the dark of night when he was alone, he questioned God. I'm sure when my brother and I were out of earshot, he and my mom would go over and over the consequences of picking up and moving again. But as a child, I never heard any shakiness in his voice. When God said, "Go," my dad went. His actions taught my brother and me that if He was moving you on, He had something better for you, and you needed to get to it as soon as you could.

When I read about Moses and the Israelites, I imagine Moses's voice much like my own father's: steady, firm, loving, sure. Moses responded to the questioning Israelites by saying,

> *Fear not, stand firm, and see the salvation of the Lord, which he will work for you today. For the Egyptians whom you see today, you shall never see again. The Lord will fight for you, and you have only to be silent.*
>
> *(Exodus 14:13–14)*

God's purpose for the Israelites was exactly what His purpose is for you: moving you to His salvation, to the freedom He created for you. Any time the Lord takes you into a wilderness season, it is because He is moving you closer to His will for your life. Don't you want to get to these things as quickly as you possibly can?

My dad had the unfortunate experiences, in two of the places where he ministered, of staying too long at one and leaving too soon from the other. He would tell you that in both of those circumstances, the pain of not listening to God was quite unbearable. He has mentioned, throughout the years, tough situations he felt happened because of his missing God's timing. In one place where he felt he stayed too long, there began to be rifts within our immediate family unit. These were tough years for my parents and me personally. During the time he felt he'd moved on too quickly, well, I can honestly say he has never stopped missing the people he ministered to there, and in many ways, he has chased the depth of relationships we built there everywhere he's been since.

> Any time the Lord takes you into a wilderness season, it is because He is moving you closer to His will for your life.

Did the Lord still use those seasons for His glory? Yes. Does He need you to follow Him in exact time in order for His ultimate will to happen? No. He is God, and He will do what He wants to do, when He wants to do it. *But don't you want to be a part of the perfect timing?* This

81

brings me to my next subject, that all-encompassing Red Sea moment in the middle of the wilderness.

Expecting God

Moses went into the wilderness knowing God was beckoning him to go there. He asked the people of Israel to trust him while also inviting them to listen for the Lord. Just as they were fleeing Egypt and then being pursued by Pharaoh's army, Moses reminded them that the fight they were in was the Lord's fight. They might have been encapsulated in the middle of it, but they must only be still and let Him fight for them. Much easier said than done, but what relief to know that such an insurmountable fortress of fear was God's to rumble with, not theirs.

Moses knew he would find God in the wilderness. He may not have been sure exactly how or when, but he knew the Lord would be there. Have you walked into your wilderness times with that same knowledge? Did you know God would be there? Or were you like the Israelites, needing proof and unsure what might be waiting for you in the wilderness?

If we are honest, we all probably hope He will be in the middle of our uncertain times, but we are a little gunshy in believing He will actually arrive. I remember when

I was a little bit older and we were making another move, I asked my dad, "How do you know for sure we should do this?" His response was, "I just trust the Lord is there waiting on me." Again, my dad had such blind trust. So much like Noah, so much like Moses; this trust that stands firm when the wind blows strong. To witness this kind of trust in person was truly astounding.

Moses expected God in his wilderness, and it completely changed his ability to navigate that uncertain time with determination and confidence.

The Red Sea moment in the wilderness was when God showed everyone present that He was, in fact, there all along. As Pharaoh's army was approaching, the Israelites were pinned between Egypt and the Red Sea. They had nowhere to go except to cross the sea. The people of Israel cried out to Moses as *he* cried out to God. And the Lord responded:

> *"Why do you cry to me? Tell the people of Israel to go forward. Lift up your staff, and stretch out your hand over the sea and divide it, that the people of Israel may go through the sea on dry ground."*
>
> *(Exodus 14:15–16)*

Right in the middle of the scariest, most uncertain, desperate time of the wilderness journey, God showed the people He had been with them all along and had, in fact, given them the power to overcome their enemy. He allowed the people of Israel to bear witness to one of the greatest acts possible from the Almighty God. He allowed Moses to part an entire sea all the way to the dry ground beneath it.

Think about this for a minute. The floor of the sea is not dry. It has tons of water sitting on top of it. Think about any time you have stepped in the ocean and felt the sand beneath your toes. It's thick, and your feet sink into it. So not only did God part the waters, but He also made the ground dry beneath them so they could walk right through.

Notice, the Lord didn't take the Israelites away from the scene where the trouble was happening; He altered the scene itself, making it perfect for their victory. God most often doesn't snatch you out of your waiting period just because tough times are closing in on you; He joins you in the midst of it and shows you who He is.

The Israelites needed proof that God had not only sent them on this seemingly forsaken journey, but that He was with them the whole time. What better way than to part a sea so they could walk through and escape their enemy?

Think about your wilderness. Where has God shown up? And if you aren't sure whether He has yet, keep looking for Him. If nothing else, acknowledge His sustaining of you in the midst of waiting. If you look for the Lord, rather than looking for the end, it makes the journey easier and much more fulfilling.

The total time in the wilderness would add up to forty years for the Israelites. God showed up in many ways over those years, testing their trust and shaping them into the people He had always wanted to inherit the promised land. Some of the Israelites never made it to the promised land. Even Moses, with all his determination and might, never made it fully there, but God let him see it from afar before he passed away.

Friend, you never know when this period of waiting in the wilderness will end. The "wilderness" for you means something different than the person next to you. One person reading this relates to these truths in a completely different manner than you do. This is the greatness and vastness of our God; His promises and purposes are for us all, no matter where we are.

Look for Him in the midst of the waiting, not just at the end. His presence is not marked by the end of

> God most often doesn't snatch you out of your waiting period just because tough times are closing in on you; He joins you in the midst of it and shows you who He is.

the waiting, but by peace within the journey. As author Martin K.M. said in a blog post about waiting: "God will test you in many ways, but the biggest test is time."[9] Moses and his people were tested at every turn, but the largest obstacle to overcome was the time it would take to receive the Lord's promises.

You can do this, friend. You can do hard things, even if they feel overwhelming and never-ending. Why? Because He is there *with* you and there *waiting on you.*

SIX

Waiting FOR YOUR FUTURE

The two most important days in your life
are the day you were born
and the day you find out why.

—Author unknown[10]

Do you know what you are supposed to do with your life? Do you already know your place within God's kingdom? Or are you still waiting for Him to show you? Do you dream of doing something great for the Lord and you feel He hasn't allowed it to happen yet?

What is it you dream of doing with your life? How does it fulfill a need of the people around you and help you live out your faith?

Your purpose in life will be where the needs of the world, your talents, and God's will meet.

This statement is true of everyone, and this was most definitely true of David, who would one day be known as King David. David had dreams, but he really had no idea that his dreams were nowhere near touching the surface of what the Lord had in store for him. You know David most likely because of his role in the "David and Goliath" story. But that story is one small snippet of the waiting period toward his destiny. Just imagine, God had such big things for him that fighting a giant was a small part of his story. Yowza.

> Your purpose in life will be where the needs of the world, your talents, and God's will meet.

I spent many years as a college minister in Nashville, Tennessee, where I now live with my family. My own personal experience can attest to the ebbs and flows of longing for God's will to take shape in your life—both when you are just starting out as an adult and in the rest of your adult life. However, my time working with young adults afforded me a front-row seat to many journeys to find the Lord's purpose in someone's life. This time can feel like the wait that never ends.

Wrapped up in waiting for your future are the swirling decisions of where to live, what friendships to continue cultivating, what job to take, how long to stay at said job, if it's okay to take a job as a bridge to what you really want to do, what grad school to go to, if you go to grad school at all. You wonder when you will meet someone to marry and why you are not married yet. You ask yourself, *Why am I the only one who doesn't have it all together?*

It's a lot. I've heard a million versions of all of those statements and questions. I probably said a few versions of those statements myself. The one concept I continued to pour into my students was this, "There is a place in God's kingdom that *only you* can fill. If that is the case, you will not accidentally miss His calling."

I wanted my students to know that God's kingdom needs a lot of jobs filled, and He has specially picked each of them to fill a role that no one else can. All the questions that lead us to worrying about our futures can leave us feeling hopeless, as if we will miss the boat while everyone else rides off into a picture-perfect sunset.

In the age of social media, the little squares perfectly curated for the public's consumption is what adds gasoline to this (already intense) flame burning inside of us. We can't help but think that "they" have it all. They have the perfect spouse, house, job, friends, etc. We wonder, *Why has God forgotten me?*

He hasn't. This waiting period has happened for everyone. You are not alone in the waiting; in fact, you have massive loads of company, and they've been right there with you for decades upon decades upon decades.

Let's see how David navigated his waiting period from the promise of his destiny to actually receiving it.

God's Purpose in Looking Forward

Long before David was born, the battle over who would rule Israel had played out in a way that prepared David to ascend to the throne. There were many players in this story. And just as in David's story, each of our journeys are intertwined with the lives and works of everyone else's.

The Lord's work in many people's lives will lead to what He has for you. And these people help you to see His will for your life come into focus. Think back to the beginning of this book; we talked about Abraham and how the decisions he made and the direction that God had for him directly affected the story of Jacob that followed.

David is a prime example of this. God's messenger, Samuel, sought out David after a series of missteps were taken by other people who didn't serve the Lord as He had wished. Israel needed a new king, and God led Samuel right to him.

God said to Samuel in 1 Samuel 16:1:

"How long will you grieve over Saul, since I have rejected him from being king over Israel? Fill your horn with oil, and go. I will send you to Jesse the Bethlehemite, for I have provided for myself a king among his sons."

One notable thing about God here is that He asked Samuel to look forward. Even though the future was uncertain, the Lord didn't want Samuel to give any more energy to what He had said was not meant to be. The past was the past, and Samuel needed to leave it there. *Sometimes the purpose in the waiting is to move your focus from what has been to what will be.* How can we claim the wonderful promises of God and live in their greatness if all we do is look behind us at what we lost?

> Sometimes the purpose in the waiting is to move your focus from what has been to what will be.

We then see in 1 Samuel 16 that the Lord gave Samuel clear direction on where he should find the next king. So Samuel went in search of Jesse and his sons. When he arrived, he met Jesse and all of his sons except for one, assuming the king must be among them. Jesse had seven of his sons pass by Samuel, but the Lord did not confirm that any of them was the king.

> *Then Samuel said to Jesse, "Are all your sons here?" And he said, "There remains yet the youngest, but behold, he is keeping the sheep." And Samuel said to Jesse, "Send and get him, for we will not sit down till he comes here." And he sent and brought him in. Now he was ruddy and had beautiful eyes and was handsome. And the LORD said, "Arise, anoint him, for this is he." Then Samuel took the horn of oil and anointed him in the midst of his brothers. And the Spirit of the LORD rushed upon David from that day forward. And Samuel rose up and went to Ramah.*
>
> (1 Samuel 16:11–13)

Though David was anointed king when he was very young, his anointing did not mean he became king immediately. Saul was still ruling, and it would take time for his reign to end. God was going to take David and the people of Israel through a lot of other tests before David would finally become king.

Scripture shows us that after David was anointed, he went right back to the sheep he was shepherding. He didn't change course in his life; only the Lord could change the course, and the anointing was just allowing David to *see* his calling. *God was not yet filling an empty void; He was merely making a plan for the future.*

Has God ever given you a vision for your life but not immediately plucked you out of your current situation, only to fulfill the vision at just the right moment? I would say, probably every time. I know for me, I've had a dream of starting a specific nonprofit for five years, but the timing just hasn't been right yet.

This dream was inspired by my oldest son, who was born on the island of Grenada. He was raised, until he was four years old, at a children's home on the island. While this home is amazing, and these children know they are loved and cherished, there are still many things this home can't afford to give them as they grow up and move out on their own. We had the great opportunity, among multiple trips, to spend time with many of the children, who were various ages. The girls who were older and will age out of the home became some of the dearest ones to me. The island has provisions in place to help them go to school when they outgrow the home, but there were many life skills that the home's directors knew the girls were missing and would likely struggle with beyond their walls. This became important to me because my son's past is so closely connected to these girls and their futures. You see, his birth mother was once in their shoes.

I have felt in my heart for a long time that if I could find a way to bridge this gap and put tools in place to help these girls, now women, navigate their new adult lives, I would be finding a way to love a little boy's future mama the way I wish I had been able to love my son's mother.

There's a lot that has to happen to fully realize this dream: It will require conducting studies with the island and seeing what preparations are already in place, finding out how we can help strengthen what they already have, and building great relationships with the government and the local children's homes and foster care placements. And then we must put together transitional living homes where life skills can be taught in real time, where the women have a safe place to sleep, and where they can learn how to become a working part of their local economy.

I know this will happen one day, and I certainly have the creative juices flowing. I could stop everything I'm doing now and make it happen, but the Lord has shown me through my current work and life, the timing isn't right yet. I'm often frustrated that I have this vision and can do nothing with it right now. I think about all the people who would be greatly impacted by the work, and I want the work to start *now*, but God says, "Not yet."

Inevitably, every single time, my conversation with Him goes this way:

Me: "But Lord, what about that person? They need what you have laid on my heart right now! What will happen if they don't receive this now?"

God: "I know what they need and when they need it. I also know what you need and when you need it. I am taking care of them just like I take care of you."

Taking a page from David's story does my heart a lot of good. Though I want to rush ahead and fulfill all my plans right now, the Lord's timing is the linchpin to my success.

1 Samuel 16:13 tells us, "The Spirit of the LORD rushed upon David from that day forward." So we know that even though David was not immediately ascending to the throne, God was with him and keeping him for his divine appointment.

Just because He has given you a dream or a vision for something you are supposed to do, doesn't mean He is giving you this thing *right now*. God sometimes comes and anoints you for your future but then leaves you where you are to work on preparing you for the way.

You may be reading this and are frustrated with your current circumstances. You know He has called you to do something or laid a burden on your heart to do something, but He has not actively made a way yet. Rest assured, my friend, if He has called you, He is equipping you in this waiting period for the day of this promise to arise. The most comforting thing you should know in this waiting time is that the Lord is with you. Just as with David, He has rushed upon you and will not leave you in the waiting alone.

> Rest assured, my friend, if He has called you, He is equipping you in this waiting period for the day of this promise to arise.

David would go on to wait nearly fifteen years to become king. He would go through many tests and trials before ascending to the throne, all of which prepared him for what was to come. And we know from his story, the waiting season is always a time of preparation for the promises.

We can believe we're ready for the whole dream to come to fruition, but we're not often actually ready for all God has for us. To be given all you have dreamed of in one shot, or all that He has willed for you, would be too overwhelming. This waiting period prepares you for the blessings and callings to come.

God Prepares Us for Our Purpose

Most often we think of waiting as lost time. We see our time being taken away, our dreams taken away, our needs taken away, maybe even people we love taken away.

I describe this as a suspension in time. While the whole world moves on, we feel stuck in the same place. When we aren't moving forward, sitting still can feel as negative and unproductive as moving backward.

I'm sure David felt this way when he went back to the fields to tend his sheep. He had to have thought, *Lord, why would You anoint me king only to send me back to the stinky field?*

But God did something interesting with David in his time leading up to being king, and if we all look closely, it's likely happening in our waiting periods too.

The first thing I noticed was that He gave David lessons about his future. Starting in 1 Samuel 16:14, we see that Saul was struck with a harmful spirit that tormented him. He believed that if someone would play him pleasing music, he would be able to calm down and the spirit would leave him. When he asked for such a man, his servants just happened to know of a boy in a field tending sheep who played a pretty mean lyre. And wouldn't you know, that boy was David.

David went to work in Saul's court, and Saul came to love David; he even made him his armor-bearer (his right-hand man in battle). So there was David, working in the court he would one day rule, learning from the king himself. God created a scenario in which Saul needed David specifically, and under those circumstances, David learned more about the role he would one day fill.

Please note, though, scripture tells us that while David was invited to Saul's court for this reason, he was making trips back and forth to also tend the sheep. I am sure this was not easy, doing two jobs at once; but God was slowly preparing David for his future.

I imagine many of you are reading this while you are in one particular job or one particular town or one particular season of life, and you know the Lord has called you elsewhere. You do not know when, but you know He is moving you on. And maybe your frustration has only built as He has moved you on from one thing to another, especially when the other "new" thing isn't what you've been waiting for.

Can I plant this seed? Perhaps this new place, while not the last place, is preparing you for your future. I am no longer a college minister. I moved on from that job, and that transition was one of the most difficult of my life. I loved what I did. I loved those young adults more than I would ever be able to express. Being a part of their lives for any amount of time was something I held as the biggest honor.

I knew about eight months before I quit that God was trying to move me on. I begged with Him. I pleaded with Him. I asked that He make another way. I did not want to leave my job. I would find myself praying before beginning my weekly lessons with the group, telling God how much I loved this work and asking Him why He would want me to leave it. Although I was never met with an audible answer, He answered me in how the details of my job changed. As my time to leave drew nearer, aspects of the job began to sour for me, aspects I once held dear. Things I looked forward to doing before became dreadful tasks. The inspiration I felt as I taught for so many years was suddenly much heavier to carry. I was so confused, but more than anything, I wanted to not feel the emotions I was feeling. I believe the Lord began to do this on purpose, to ensure I moved on.

That job absolutely was preparing me for the next thing; God was *giving* me what I needed for the future. And when I look back, I know now that my entire time spent in college ministry was preparing me for what I'm doing now.

David's time in Saul's court taught him the lessons he needed to learn as the future king. There was no better crash course than one in the very court in which he would one day serve.

> If any of you lacks wisdom, let him ask God, who gives generously to all without reproach, and it will be given him. (James 1:5)

What is this current season giving to you that is preparing you for the next? If you aren't sure, ask God to show you. He desires for you to know your purpose and live in it with certainty for His kingdom. Ask Him, friend, and He will give you clarity and knowledge.

As a side note, the Bible points out that if you ask the Lord, He will give you wisdom. James 1:5 says, "If any of you lacks wisdom, let him ask God, who gives generously to all without reproach, and it will be given him." He is not hiding this from you, He wants you to know your purpose and the purpose of this season for you.

David's waiting period here offered several opportunities to show what the past had prepared him for. So first we saw God point David toward the future, then He had David reflect on his past. David was going to be thrown into the fight of his life, but God had prepared him for this moment long before it would happen.

1 Samuel 17 recounts the famous story we all know so well, in which David slayed the giant Goliath. The Philistines had come to battle, and they wanted a man to fight their best soldier, their champion, Goliath. Many days of fighting ensued with no one brave enough to defeat the man, described as "a man of war from his youth" (verse 33). David went out to take provisions to his brothers, who were soldiers in the battle, and he saw the dilemma the soldiers were facing. He questioned why Goliath would even challenge the armies of the Lord, and his gusto made its way all the way to Saul. 1 Samuel 17:31–37 recounts Saul and David's exchange:

> *When the words that David spoke were heard, they repeated them before Saul, and he sent for him. And David said to Saul, "Let no man's heart fail because of him. Your servant will go and fight with*

this Philistine." And Saul said to David, "You are not able to go against this Philistine to fight with him, for you are but a youth, and he has been a man of war from his youth." But David said to Saul, "Your servant used to keep sheep for his father. And when there came a lion, or a bear, and took a lamb from the flock, I went after him and struck him and delivered it out of his mouth. And if he arose against me, I caught him by his beard and struck him and killed him. Your servant has struck down both lions and bears, and this uncircumcised Philistine shall be like one of them, for he has defied the armies of the living God." And David said, "The LORD who delivered me from the paw of the lion and from the paw of the bear will deliver me from the hand of this Philistine." And Saul said to David, "Go, and the LORD be with you!"

David saw the problem that lay ahead for the Israelites, and God pricked his heart to affirm that he was, in fact, a man positioned to help them. David was then able to recount for Saul the ways he was prepared to help, so that he could be sent into battle.

In your waiting period, you will face challenges. You will face moments of uncertainty, moments of doubt, moments of pain, and moments of fear. Just as God is giving you lessons about your future, He is also giving you confidence in the road ahead. Just as He did with David. *He is showing you that what He has already placed inside of you is enough to take hold of the promises He has for you.* Instead of looking at this time as being "taken" from you, see these moments as "giving" you the lessons you need and the confidence you desire to move forward to your future. He is preparing you for greatness because He has already made you great. Walk in that knowledge today.

These things I have mentioned are small potatoes in the large meal of trials David would face as he waited to become king of Israel. And once he did become king, he became king of Judah and then still had to wait to become king over all of Israel. He had to have patience that the anointing, the promise, God had made to him when he was a boy would come to fruition. David had to trust that God was true to His word and that in His timing, he would become all that God had said He would be.

> You have to trust that the Lord's promises are not watered down or erased by time.

You have to trust that the Lord's promises are not watered down or erased by time. If He has promised it, it will come

103

to be. You have to trust that if He has called you to something, if He has prepared something for you, there is no one and nothing that can get in the way of it. Author, evangelist, and speaker Christine Caine says, "God is preparing you for the place that He has prepared for you."[11] I love this reminder of what He is doing in each of our lives for an appointed time.

The throne was David's. No one could change that, no matter how long it took David to finally sit on the throne.

The same is true for you, my friend. If God has prepared a place for you, it is yours alone. *God's will for you will not disappear because "you didn't make it on time." This is not a thing.* That space, that place, that person, that job, that town—whatever it is—it is yours, no matter how long it takes you to get there.

SEVEN

Waiting FOR YOUR TROUBLES TO PASS

> I have said these things to you, that in me you may
> have peace. In the world you will have tribulation. But
> take heart; I have overcome the world.
>
> —*John 16:33*

I f you've ever read the book of Job in the Old Testament, you've maybe been like me and thought, *There is no chance this all happened to one guy.* Job's story is riddled with pain and loss and hardship, yet he was a man after the Lord's heart. Ever heard it said that, "God will not give you more than you can handle"? This story, I think, disproves that idea: Job definitely got his fair share and then some.

For each of us, the word *troubles* means something different. I know people who have endured chronic pain their whole lives and have never found a cure. I know people who had a loved one massively hurt in an accident that changed their life's course in a matter of seconds. I know people who have had to bury their children. I know people who have to share custody of their children with someone who is very difficult to reason with while also navigating a messy divorce. I know people who have lost their jobs a long time ago and have gone years without finding the right work to dive back into. And as I'm writing, I know people who have been cut off from family members because of sickness and illness, and many people have been isolated from the people they love the most.

Your troubles could be anything you've read about in previous chapters, or they could be completely different. If you are going through a season where nothing seems to go right, I pray this chapter meets you exactly where the wound is bleeding. And if your troublesome season has passed, I pray this chapter helps remind you of what God did during that time to help you walk forward in confidence of *who He is* and what He said He would do for you.

The book of Job tells us of a man who was blameless in the eyes of the Lord. This didn't mean he was sinless, but that he was a man of integrity who consistently and sincerely loved God, upheld His Word, and resisted evil. Satan approached God and wanted to "test" Job's faith, for Satan believed the only reason Job loved and obeyed the Lord so much was because He had given him too much. The man had it all—wealth, success, family (see Job 1:1– 5). Was he only this way because God blessed him? And did he only serve Him because of all he'd been given?

> *Then Satan answered the* Lord *and said, "Does Job fear God for no reason? Have you not put a hedge around him and his house and all that he has, on every side? You have blessed the work of his hands, and his possessions have increased in the land. But stretch out your hand and touch all that he has, and he will curse you to your face." And the* Lord *said to Satan, "Behold, all that he has is in your hand. Only against him do not stretch out your hand." So, Satan went out from the presence of the* Lord.
>
> *(Job 1:9–12)*

Satan wanted to see if Job's love for and faithfulness to God was genuine. And the Lord allowed this with one condition, essentially saying, "You can touch anything he owns or has, but you cannot harm Job himself." And so, Satan's game began. Let's dive into Job's story, which is not written so much as an obvious story of waiting, but a tale of suffering and woes that seem unimaginable to live through. His is a story of waiting for troubles to pass.

First, Satan attacked Job's property, animals, and children. He slayed all the animals, destroyed all the property, and killed Job's children. You can find the full description of these terrible acts in Job 1:13–19. Job replied by tearing his clothing, shaving his head, and falling to the ground to worship God. With all that hardship falling on him at once, he still didn't denounce his love for God. Can you imagine? Job didn't even question what God was doing or what he had done to deserve the heartache.

> Often, because we associate good with God, labeling something "bad" as coming from Him doesn't compute. But if we are willing to accept all the good, should we not also be willing to accept what we deem bad?

Second, Satan attacked Job's health, giving him painful sores from the bottom of his feet all the way to the top of his head. After all that suffering, his wife asked him why he would not curse the Lord, and Job replied, in Job 2:10, "You speak as one of the foolish women would speak.

Shall we receive good from God, and shall we not receive evil?" He still would not speak ill of Him.

Job made an astounding point. Often, because we associate good with God, labeling something "bad" as coming from Him doesn't compute. But if we are willing to accept all the good, should we not also be willing to accept what we deem bad?

Job didn't really know if the "bad" things were directly from the Lord, but he trusted Him completely and assumed He was at least allowing it to happen for a reason. And if this were the case, he must accept it in stride. Job showed tremendous faith in the Lord with his assurance that the Lord knew best for him at all turns. And sometimes, what's best for us is the love from our friends. (And sometimes, well, it isn't.)

God's Purpose in Who Shows Up

If you continue to read the book of Job, you'll find in chapters 3–37 that Job was visited by three friends, Eliphaz, Bildad, and Zophar, who had heard of his troubles and came to offer support. Literally, for thirty-five chapters Job commiserated with his friends Eliphaz, Bildad, and Zophar. They had heard of his troubles and went to offer some comfort; at least that's how the Bible describes their reasoning for visiting Job.

You've commiserated with your friends too. You've done this. You know you've done this. I know I've done this. Many a pint of ice cream never made it past my worldly troubles, and the spoons I used can attest to this, so I can't lie. Digging into a pint of ice cream is my equivalent to thirty-five chapters of talking.

Job's friends sat and mourned with him for seven days and seven nights, no one speaking the entire time. And then, once he began to talk, they each put their "two cents in," sharing their own beliefs about why he was suffering like he was. They each had different opinions, but the most prominent was that Job must have done something (sinned) to have brought the troubles on himself. The bottom line of each of their "speeches" was that Job needed to repent to the Lord so that he could get his life back on track.

One of the things noted by Henrietta Mears in *What the Bible Is All About*[12] is that at least Job's friends came to him and didn't desert him. When troubles hit a person from all sides, often people choose to stay away, to even abandon a friend, because they're uncomfortable being close to pain and difficulty. But not all of Job's friends did this. He had four come to his side during that time (we'll talk about that fourth friend shortly).

Maybe you are going through something and you feel like some of the people you needed the most have not been there. What I've often found is that we abandon when we don't know how to show up. If we aren't sure what someone needs, we tend to not give at all. Let this be a lesson for all of us—even if you don't know what to give, just make yourself available, and give your presence. "Companionable silence" is what I call it. We all need that from time to time, especially when life gets thick and tough.

Job's friends, well . . . they are each a piece of work in their own right. They start off the right way, with companionable silence, but they soon move to giving their own opinions of what they think Job should do. These friends didn't get everything right, but they did add so much to the story here. I submit to you that *sometimes the purpose of your tough times is for those around you as much, if not more, than it is for you.*

> Sometimes He is doing a work for your friends through your life and sometimes He is doing a work for you through your friends' responses to your circumstances.

I believe Job's friends learned a lot about God and how He works in our lives by watching Job's circumstances.

Sometimes He is doing a work for your friends through your life, *and* sometimes He is doing a work for you through your friends' responses to your circumstances.

Both of these scenarios played out in Job's story. Seeing Job's faith lived out in such a real and vulnerable way had to make a lasting impact on the friends who stuck by him. And if Job didn't make an impact on them, in the end, God sure was going to make an impact Himself.

First, Eliphaz noted that Job had been a man who had encouraged many, so how could he fold in the face of adversity? He said in Job 4:5–6, "But now it has come to you, and you are impatient; it touches you, and you are dismayed. Is not your fear of God your confidence, and the integrity of your ways your hope?"

Eliphaz was reminding Job of the man he had always been in an un-swayed world. Now that trouble had come to Job, Eliphaz pleaded with him to continue in the integrity of his ways because that trait had encouraged Eliphaz in the past. Job was taking his eyes off of God, who had sustained him in the good times. Eliphaz rebuked Job for being impatient when troubles hit him personally. He was being a hypocrite, and Eliphaz wanted him to see that.

It is so easy for us to lose sight of who we are and what we believe in when trouble hits. However, those closest to us remember the things about us that have inspired them, and if given the opportunity, they will encourage us to keep those traits in our darkest hours.

Job's next friend to chime in was Bildad. He was a real piece of work. Bildad began by arguing his point confidently, wishing Job to confess his sin because that must have been why Job was in his position. However, what I love most about Bildad's persistence is the end of his first conversation in Job 8:20–22 when he said, "Behold, God will not reject a blameless man, nor take the hand of evil-doers. He will yet fill your mouth with laughter, and your lips with shouting. Those who hate you will be clothed with shame, and the tent of the wicked will be no more."

I believe that even though Bildad spent most of his time pushing Job to repent of his sinful ways, he was also taking those moments to reinforce what he knew and loved about Job. He reminded Job of who he was and what God wanted for him. Remember in Job 1:1, we find out that Job was blameless in the eyes of the Lord. The blameless man he was in the past was still the man he was that day, and Bildad wanted him to know that God longed to bring joy back into his life.

The next friend, Zophar, told it like it was. He showed Job that although he had come upon so much trouble in his life, we as humans deserve much worse than what

Job had been given. Wow! I am sure Job received this encouragement so well. I know I would just adore someone who looked upon my troubles and said, "Yeah, well you deserve more." My dad calls this the "spiritual gift of encouragement." You know these people; they give stinging advice cloaked by "Christian concern."

And to that I say, "Blah. Go away." There may have been truth to what Zophar was saying, but now was not the time my friend, not the time. I'm sure that is how Job felt with Zophar. But then Zophar said in Job 11:16–17, "You will forget your misery; you will remember it as waters that have passed away. And your life will be brighter than the noonday; its darkness will be like the morning."

> Find yourself a friend who will speak truth to you even when it's difficult to hear, someone who will encourage you that God will not end your story in meaninglessness.

Look at you, Zophar! Maybe you aren't so bad. He was giving Job hope for the future. He knew that sinners deserved so much worse, but he showed Job that "this too shall pass," and that one day it would all be a memory of what God had brought him through. Find yourself a friend who will speak truth to you even when it's difficult to hear, someone who will encourage you that God will not end your story in mean-inglessness. He always has a plan, and it will be bright like "the noonday."

If you continue to read the book of Job, you will see how the Lord didn't love the advice these three friends gave. In chapter 42, He rebuked their advice, because it didn't accurately represent what He would say. And this is a good reminder that while our advice can be good and helpful sometimes, we have to be careful when we speak *for God*.

However, what I can say is this: At least they showed up and tried to give what they could to Job. Their efforts may have fallen short of what Job needed to get out of the pit he was in, but they at least tried. This is what I meant earlier about when we are afraid to show up for people because getting close to pain and suffering isn't something we want to do. But even if our feeble efforts fall short of God's best, He is the One who redeems those actions.

If you know someone facing troubles, just show up. You don't have to have the answers or the right words. Be present, and be a silent support beside them while they toil.

Expecting God

After many back-and-forth conversations with Job, Eliphaz, Bildad, and Zophar, we finally meet one more friend named Elihu. I mean seriously, haven't we heard enough already? But this friend will be different.

(Also, a side note, I am so glad my friends have easier names, such as Kathryn or Lauren or Nora. Even Kelsie and Monica and Casey are better. It's much easier to write their names. Job's friends' names have been a trip to type.)

Elihu was frustrated with Job's previous three friends because they didn't "fix" Job's problems. Elihu pointed out that Job was trying to justify himself with how good *he* was rather than extolling how wonderful *God* was. His rant ended with speaking of the greatness and majesty of the Lord. He pointed Job's eyes upward and told Job to trust in Him.

> The purpose in your waiting may be to bring together believers who share in their suffering and can point each other to the Lord so that His love can be seen through the tragedy.

What a friend to have, one who will point you to God in hard times. Elihu showed that the purpose in your waiting is not always for you alone. The purpose in your waiting may be to bring together believers who share in their suffering and can point each other to the Lord so that His love can be seen through the tragedy. He has not left you. He has not forsaken you. He needs your life, and your willingness to live it, to be a testimony to those around you.

I am so grateful for the relatable example God gives us in Job's friends. I'm sure you can think of the most difficult time you have gone through—or are currently experiencing—and remember who showed up for you. We don't forget those who didn't shy away from the pain and heartache just because it was uncomfortable.

Being uncomfortable with tough things is normal. It's human of us to shy away from others' pain. However, showing up for someone is even tougher and far more memorable. It's an act that resonates for a lifetime.

As firm as Job was in his foundation with God, when tested on all sides, he was still human and questioned his place within His economy. Job's friends came to him in his hour of need, and though all of them may not have left the impressions God hoped for, one friend helped him recognize what (or *whom*) the Lord had been wanting him to see: God Himself amid all the troubles.

When you for one second take your eyes off of the Lord, you want the person standing next to you to lift your chin back up to the heavens. This gives the ole, "Keep your chin up, kid" a whole new meaning.

As thankful as I am for Job's friends, I can't help but find one thing particularly disheartening: They talked amongst themselves for thirty-five chapters. THIRTY-FIVE chapters. They rambled and squabbled and commiserated and argued for *thirty-five* chapters.

Think about this. How often do we hit hard times and go whine to our friends or the closest willing ear? We look for someone to resonate with our misery, to wallow in it with us, before we ever go to God. It is so natural, and way easier, to look for the approval and confirmation of friends and their opinions rather than going to God in prayer. This is especially true if we are angry with Him for our circumstances. But we often forget that God is a big boy; He can take our anger.

After thirty-five chapters, God talked directly to Job, saying, "Where were you when I laid the foundation of the earth?"

Boom! I am the God of ALL. I made everything long before you were even here. I have made everything and given everything its place and time and rhythm, and you dare question My reasoning for you as one small part of this realm?!

Later, the Lord said to Job in chapter 40 verse 2, "Shall a faultfinder contend with the Almighty? He who argues with God, let him answer it." I think at this point I would have peed my pants. Who wants to argue with the Almighty?

Friend, if you are looking for the end of your troubles, please know, *there is no end to troubles without Jesus.* You can reason and ask and squabble with any and everyone under the sun to try to make sense of your plight; but if you do not have God in your life, there will be no end to your troubles.

We must turn our eyes back to Him. Lift up our chins and gaze to the heavens. Have you ever noticed if you turn your head upward all the way and move your eyes in every direction possible, you can only see the heavens? Sure, maybe you can see the top of the tree next to you, or the top of the wall in the room you are in; but you can't see all that lies on the ground around you or what work your hands are trying to accomplish. You can only see the heavens.

Looking for "the end" of this circumstance in life is dragging your eyes down. Keep your chin up, kid. Look for the Lord, and you will find the joy that will carry you until the end.

EIGHT

Waiting FOR DELIVERANCE

God found Gideon in a hole.
He found Joseph in a prison.
He found Daniel in a lion's den.
He has a curious habit of showing up in the midst of trouble, not the absence. Where the world sees failure, God sees future.
Next time you feel unqualified to be used by God remember this, he tends to recruit from the pit, not the pedestal.

—*Jon Acuff,* New York Times *best-selling author and motivational speaker*[13]

A quick Google search will give the definition of *deliverance* as "the action of being rescued or set free." Waiting to be "delivered" is something we likely feel in every waiting season. You might be thinking, after reading the previous seven chapters, "Yeah, Krystal, I'm waiting to be delivered from the waiting."

This definition has a particular meaning, one that implies bondage to a situation. My opinion about the Lord's "waiting periods" in your life is that they are not bondage at all; they are moments that help expose the freedom we have in Christ. I say this because God gives us a specific story about deliverance in the sixth chapter of the book of Daniel. I believe this example illustrates something about being delivered that these other waiting periods do not.

> My opinion about the Lord's "waiting periods" in your life is that they are not bondage at all; they are moments that help expose the freedom we have in Christ.

Let's set the stage a bit so you know where Daniel is when we find him in chapter 6. Daniel served the kingdom of Babylon. Darius, the king at the time, decided to make a new hierarchy in which three people would be the high officials; Daniel would be one of the three. Then the Bible tells us in Daniel 6:3: "Then this Daniel became distinguished above all the other high officials and satraps, because an excellent spirit was in him. And the king planned to set him over the whole kingdom."

The remaining two people who would make up this new hierarchy began to complain, because they didn't want Daniel to be in charge. Basically, jealousy reared its ugly head. They began to try to find fault in Daniel, and when they could not, they decided that the fault must be with the God Daniel served. The easiest way to accomplish this was to persuade the king to enact a law that no one should be allowed to pray to anyone other than Darius himself. The punishment if anyone was found worshipping someone else . . . the lions' den. Daniel's response?

When Daniel knew that the document had been signed, he went to his house where he had windows in his upper chamber open toward Jerusalem. He got down on his knees three times a day and prayed and gave thanks before his God, as he had done previously.
                                                                                (Daniel 6:10)

He continued doing exactly as he had done previously. Wow! I think it's plain and simple that this was a man who would not be swayed by mankind and their self-serving rules. So, of course, his conspirators trapped him in his prayer time and reported him to the king. Darius, who genuinely loved Daniel, hesitated for a moment. He tried to see if there was a way to *not* punish Daniel, but as with most conspirators, these guys were clever. They told the king in Daniel 6:15, "Know, O king, that it is a law of the Medes and Persians that no injunction or ordinance that the king establishes can be changed."

Once they had urged Darius to make the law to throw people in the den of lions, they wanted to ensure he couldn't change his mind just for how he felt about Daniel. So the king listened to the men and commanded they throw Daniel to the lions. He said to Daniel in verse 6:16, "May your God, whom you serve continually, deliver you!" before sealing him in. Darius was not well after his decision. He didn't sleep all night. Then, when he returned to see the fate of Daniel the next morning, this exchange happened:

> As he came near to the den where Daniel was, he cried out in a tone of anguish. The king declared to Daniel, "O Daniel, servant of the living God, has your God, whom you serve continually, been able to deliver you from the lions?" Then Daniel said to the king, "O king, live forever! My God sent his angel and shut the lions' mouths, and they have not harmed me, because I was found blameless before him; and also before you, O king, I have done no harm." Then the king was exceedingly glad, and commanded that Daniel be taken up out of the den. So Daniel was

taken up out of the den, and no kind of harm was
found on him, because he had trusted in his God.
(Daniel 6:20–23)

This may seem like a weird story to cover in the midst of talking about waiting, but not all waiting periods are long. Some are short but packed with God's promises.

Daniel's short waiting period is one of the most famous we have. Why? Because Daniel's actions magnified the traits of the Lord in one of the largest ways we can possibly witness.

God's Purpose in the Lions' Den

Sometimes the sole purpose in our waiting is for God's glory to be revealed, and this was most certainly the purpose of Daniel's jaunt in the den of lions. As we read before, the king yelled down to see if Daniel's God had saved him. And we see Daniel reply in verses 21 and 22, "O king, live forever! My God sent his angel and shut the lions' mouths, and they have not harmed me, because I was found blameless before him; and also before you, O king, I have done no harm."

Friend, with God as your Savior, no person or difficult period of time can harm you. You are set apart for His glory. For Daniel, thankfully, his deliverance came quickly. After seeing that Daniel was unharmed and requesting he be removed from the den, King Darius sent out a decree:

Then King Darius wrote to all the peoples, nations, and languages that dwell in all the earth: "Peace be multiplied to you. I make a decree, that in all my royal dominion people are to tremble and fear before the God of Daniel,

for he is the living God,
enduring forever;
his kingdom shall never be destroyed,
and his dominion shall be to the end.
He delivers and rescues;
he works signs and wonders
in heaven and on earth,
he who has saved Daniel
from the power of the lions."

(Daniel 6:25–27)

God's power and glory and majesty were on display for Darius through the act of Daniel's waiting and willingness to trust in Him. When the Lord's majesty shines, anyone who witnesses it can't help but acknowledge Him and His truth. This is what happened for Darius; he could not ignore the power of God when he saw it. His purpose in our waiting is so those around us can see His majesty on display. The work He has done for us, in even the most difficult of times, is what He longs to do for everyone else, as well. This is a way for others to see God through the testimony of our lives.

God's Perfect Peace

I fully believe that to find peace in the middle of life's lions' den, you must be the kind of person who continually seeks peace in all other areas of life. What you plant is what you grow, right? If you plant seeds of peace and faith, peace and faith will sprout up. It's most certainly what will come out when you are pressed on all sides.

I've found time and time again that when I sow peace and faith into my life on a daily basis, when tough times hit me, those gems sprout up to give me strength.

We can see this theme in Daniel's life. He had been

> I've found time and time again that when I sow peace and faith into my life on a daily basis, when tough times hit me, those gems sprout up to give me strength.

brought to Babylon (many years before Darius took the throne), against his will, to help grow the kingdom being established there. Daniel 1 describes how faithful Daniel was and how proud he was of his work, despite his circumstances. He had made peace with his position, and we can see this by the quality and nature of the work he produced.

In Daniel 6, we have the hullabaloo with Darius and his conspirators. When Daniel heard about Darius's new law, he just continued about what he was doing, praising the Lord. He continued on in peace as if nothing was going on around him.

Then we come to the den of lions. We don't see Daniel's emotions when they came to throw him into the den. If he fought or cried out or anything like that, the scripture doesn't relay it. However, when the king went to look in on him the next morning, the first thing I notice is his peace. His first words to Darius in Daniel 6:21 were "Oh king, live forever!" You can only answer in that way to a king—who was a trusted friend, no less—who has thrown you to your death if you have peace in your heart, soul, and spirit.

I feel like Daniel was literally dripping peace from his sweat glands. It just oozed from him. It would have had to have been in order for him to peacefully navigate the lots thrown at him.

The definitions of *peace* are vast, but two of them that stuck out to me when I Googled it were: "Freedom from disturbance; tranquility" and "A state or period in which there is no war or a war has ended."

Just think about a life lived free of disturbance and full of tranquility. Imagine a world or a heart wherein there is no war. This was the state I believe God allowed Daniel to live in to afford him to successfully navigate waiting for deliverance.

What about you? Do you have peace? If not, ask God to give you peace so that when you need deliverance, your peace will carry you through.

NINE

Waiting ON THE WORLD TO CHANGE

I'm curious how often you've read the book of Habakkuk. Like every week, right? Yeah, thought so. Habakkuk is not only an interesting name to say, but a book I have found is not too often visited.

His book is one of history and prophecy. He wrote in a time when nations were fighting and falling. Throughout the text, Habakkuk was beyond stressed and looking for the ultimate peace we talked about Daniel having.

Strife surrounded Habakkuk. He looked out at his nation of Judah and all the evil, and he felt the Lord was

silent. He wanted to know why He was not interven-
ing among so much hurt and turmoil. Sound familiar?
Present day, anyone?

Instead of being frustrated with God and running
from Him, Habakkuk decided to have a conversation
with Him. And that conversation is what the entire book
of Habakkuk is all about.

Habakkuk began with a lament:

> O LORD, how long shall I cry for help,
>   and you will not hear?
> Or cry to you "Violence!"
>   and you will not save?
> Why do you make me see iniquity,
>   and why do you idly look at wrong?
> Destruction and violence are before me;
>   strife and contention arise.
> So the law is paralyzed,
>   and justice never goes forth.
> For the wicked surround the righteous;
>   so justice goes forth perverted.
>
> *(Habakkuk 1:1–4)*

We aren't totally sure how long Habakkuk had been
pleading with the Lord to show up and help. We don't
know exactly how many days and nights he had spent

praying to Him. We do know, however, that it must have been a significant amount of time if he began this letter of longing with, "How long shall I cry for help?" Typically, you wouldn't say that after asking just once.

But just like all of us, Habakkuk couldn't see the whole picture. God was working behind the scenes, and there was a lot to come that would alter the course of time and ultimately answer Habakkuk's prayers. You see, God's timing is not our timing, and Habakkuk was about to receive a formal lesson in this.

God's Purpose in Turmoil

As I write this book, America is in another presidential election year. These years are the most polarizing and most volatile years we ever live through. I imagine other countries are the same. People who normally live in complete harmony start baring their sharp teeth once they know you may not agree with them politically. It's honestly the most disheartening thing to watch.

As a parent, I want my child to understand the political process and the goodness it affords our country when done well. This year, I wasn't able to let my son watch much of the candidates' debating for all the vitriol. As I sat in front of the TV one night and watched two grown men yell at each other, I turned the volume down and asked my son to go to his room. This was no longer educational; it was mean-spirited, and I didn't need my child seeing grown people act in a way I will not allow him to act.

My mind drifted to September 11, 2001, the day our nation was attacked and a war began. That was the day I began to see politicians immerse themselves in every aspect of our lives. (It had certainly happened before, but as a teenager, this was the first time I would recognize it.) Though there had been many wars prior to this, I'd only read about them, but this one, I would live through. This was the war I would remember for my lifetime.

However, as much as I listened to the news and commentators arguing over whose method was right and whose was wrong, I never had to live in an active war zone. I wasn't dodging bullets and shrapnel. But somewhere, a girl my age in another country was doing just that. You see, there are multiple lenses through which people view politics and the health of their nations. As a girl who has lived through an attack on her country, but hasn't lived in a war zone, I view it completely differently than someone who had to live through both the attack *and* the war. Our friend Habakkuk was living through all of it—the politicizing, the attacking, the wars.

Historical context can be found in the Lord's answer to Habakkuk's plea:

> *"Look among the nations, and see;*
>   *wonder and be astounded.*
> *For I am doing a work in your days*
>   *that you would not believe if told.*
> *For behold, I am raising up the Chaldeans,*
>   *that bitter and hasty nation,*
> *who march through the breadth of the earth,*
>   *to seize dwellings not their own."*
>
>   *(Habakkuk 1:5–6)*

Because of his mention of the Chaldeans (another name for the Babylonians), scholars believe that Habakkuk's prophecy was written sometime in the seventh century BC, before the Babylonians invaded Judah.[15] This is what would start the movement toward the peace Habakkuk was looking for, although not as quickly as he may have liked.

It's easy for us to believe in, and hope for, a world where we get to see the full arc of God's promises and plans. However, Habakkuk's story shows us that this is not always the case. He didn't live to see the entire fulfillment of God's promise. From what we can tell, he lived long enough to see the Babylonians attack Jerusalem sometime in 597 BC. That attack was the catalyst for the reckoning Habakkuk had prayed for, one that would hold people accountable for the evil they had done and bring peace to a nation.

These timelines show us he prayed for this to happen for around twelve years. Twelve years of longing for the Lord to intervene. Twelve years of hoping God would see a world falling apart and do something about it. Twelve years of hoping, twelve years of praying, twelve years of longing, twelve years of time.

Think about your own life, and even more so, the lives of your grandparents. Were there things their generation hoped to see that took beyond their lifetime to accomplish? Most likely, yes. God works things out in His own time, and His time is not our time. As He said to Habakkuk, "I am doing a work in your days that you would not believe if told" (Habakkuk 1:5). The Lord affirmed that not only would He answer Habakkuk's prayers, but the works He would do in the nation of Jerusalem would far exceed what Habakkuk could imagine.

I can certainly attribute this feeling to my own life. My husband and I often look at our life now, three kids in a beautiful home where we're all thriving, and imagine if someone had told us on our wedding day this is where we would be. Never in a million years would we have believed it. We didn't want to have kids when we got married. I always say now, "This is all a joke!" because I was definitely the gal who was not having children. But here I am, a mom of three boys—one by adoption, two by biological birth. And prior to them, I lost three girls in the adoption process. Had you told that sweet, naive bride when she was twenty-six what her life would look like ten years later, she would have laughed at you.

God is doing a work in your life that you would not believe even if He told you all His plans right now. You don't currently have the capacity to understand it.

> Sometimes the purpose of God placing you in the middle of this waiting period is that He needs a soldier on the field who is a testament to His goodness and His coming hope.

His will is an arc that is vast and expands beyond our lifetimes, and sometimes the purpose of God placing you in the middle of this waiting period is that He needs a soldier on the field who is a testament to His goodness and His coming hope.

Habakkuk was a living testament in a tumultuous time of the goodness of God. Even though Habakkuk longed for Him to do more, he was certain He would come through. So much so that we see three times in his book where he planted his feet in faith in the middle of turmoil. See these verses throughout chapters 2 and 3:

> *I will take my stand at my watchpost and station myself on the tower, and look out to see what he will say to me, and what I will answer concerning my complaint.*
>
> *(Habakkuk 2:1)*

> *Yet I will quietly wait for the day of trouble to come upon people who invade us.*
>
> *(Habakkuk 3:16)*

> *Yet I will rejoice in the Lord; I will take joy in the God of my salvation.*
>
> *(Habakkuk 3:18)*

He had made his petitions, and he was certain the Lord would hear him and respond; he only had to patiently wait, even if his waiting was through hard times.

What steadiness of heart and firmness of spirit Habakkuk showed. My hope is for all of us to be able to pray to God for what we need and then wait patiently for His answers. So much easier said than done—but by this example, it is possible.

Habakkuk knew God and knew He would intervene *because He said He would.* He trusted in Him and therefore could attest to the goodness He would bring.

You may be blinded by everything around you. The noise from the news, social media, and your neighbors may be deafening. But know this, friend, the Lord sees all of it. None of this is catching Him off guard; none of this is surprising Him. And not only does He see it, He already has a plan for it. You, friend, are a part of His plan.

One of my favorite quotes of all time is from Gary Haugen, the founder, CEO, and former president of International Justice Mission. He said, "God has a plan to help bring justice to the world—and His plan is us."[16] We are a part of His plan. Your purpose in this waiting season is to be a soldier of His hope for those around you to see.

God Provides Peace

Habakkuk looked at his circumstances with hope in his heart. He had this hope because God made promises to him that He was working behind the scenes, even when Habakkuk couldn't see it.

He reinforced His promise in Habakkuk 2:3 saying, "For still the vision awaits its appointed time; it hastens to the end—it will not lie. If it seems slow, wait for it; it will surely come; it will not delay." The Lord wanted Habakkuk to have hope in the middle of his waiting. Therefore, He was helping Habakkuk's waiting periods give him hope for a future; *give* being the primary word here.

As I mentioned in chapter 6, so often we see our moments of waiting as taking from us. In a world where we see evil and divisive behavior at every turn, it can feel like it's stealing your joy and peace.

> *Nothing* can stop God's plan for you from happening when the time is right. *Nothing.*

Look at this verse above, friend. What hope the Lord is infusing into the waiting! He's saying that the vision He has given you is coming, but at His perfect time. The vision is not a lie. Its journey to fruition may seem slow, but when it is time for it to come, it will not delay. *Nothing* can stop God's plan for you from happening when the time is right. *Nothing.*

Habakkuk spent a long time looking for peace. He waited for the day that God would show up and bring His presence to a nation so wracked with pain. *Yet*, in the end, he praised God because he knew the promise was true: The vision for peace would not delay when the time was right.

The book ends with Habakkuk's rejoicing in the Lord even though the promise for which he had been waiting was not before his eyes yet.

> *Though the fig tree should not blossom, nor fruit be on the vines, the produce of the olive fail and the fields yield no food, the flock be cut off from the fold and there be no herd in the stalls,* **yet I will rejoice in the** LORD; **I will take joy in the God of my salvation.** *God, the Lord, is my strength; he makes my feet like the deer's; he makes me tread on my high places. To the choirmaster: with stringed instruments.*
> (Habakkuk 3:17–19, emphasis added)

The trees and flowers were not blooming. There was nothing pretty or nourishing to be found. The fruit on the vines was no longer. The fields were bare. The animals were not where they should be. *Yet*, I will rejoice in the Lord. *Yet*, I will take joy in the God of my salvation. *Yet*, God is still my strength. Habakkuk found the ways the Lord *was giving* to Him and *would continue giving* to him in the coming days, and he chose to live in the giving while he waited, rather than living in the taking.

How would your circumstances, or at least your acceptance and governance of them, change if you lived in the giving instead of the taking? Precious one, please live in the giving. There is so much life and abundance if you live in the giving of your waiting.

I heard this saying once that's resonating with me here: "The optimist sees the donut, the pessimist sees the hole."[17] Habakkuk, by his continuing conversations with God, could get a glimpse of the whole donut. He stopped seeing the hole and finally started seeing the donut.

The sad truth of Habakkuk's prayers of waiting on the world to change is that we are still waiting for the same thing. This lesson, if no other one, shows us how cyclical life is and how closely related to biblical times we actually are. Habakkuk prayed to God, "Destruction and violence are before me; strife and contention arise. So the law is paralyzed, and justice never goes forth. For the wicked surround the righteous; so justice goes forth perverted" (Habakkuk 1:3–4). I read that and think he could be talking about my country right now, today. Nothing is new under the sun, right? Habakkuk's divisions and strife are so closely related to ours. However, just as God helped Habakkuk navigate his waiting period with a renewed perspective, so too will He help us.

The same God of peace and salvation who promised to show up for Habakkuk is the same One who will show up for us.

Ask God to change your perspective. Once you do, the waiting will seem less heavy. With the current state of our nation as we attempt to elect a new president, I'm choosing to see the giving instead of the taking. The taking is everywhere around me. When I look at the taking only, it encompasses my whole view. But when I look for the giving, I see less and less of the taking.

Join me, friend. Let's live in the giving of the waiting.

TEN

Waiting FOR THE RESURRECTION, HERE AND NOW

Do not stand at my grave and weep
I am not there. I do not sleep.
I am a thousand winds that blow.
I am the diamond glints on snow.
I am the sunlight on ripened grain.
I am the gentle autumn rain.
When you awaken in the morning's hush
I am the swift uplifting rush
Of quiet birds in circled flight.
I am the soft stars that shine at night.
Do not stand at my grave and cry;
I am not there. I did not die.
—*Mary Elizabeth Frye, American poet*[18]

We wait for resurrection in many ways. There are
two kinds of resurrection: the kind we can see

here on earth—the healing kind—and the kind that will bring all of God's people home to heaven to live with Him forever.

The Lord teaches us about both in the book of John when we hear about the death of Jesus's friend Lazarus.

You typically only hear about resurrection when referencing Jesus's resurrection on Easter Sunday or the resurrection of God's people in His second coming. However, in the Bible we get to see a time that God resurrected someone from the dead, and through this story, I believe that He shows us a lot about Himself and His will for us when we feel dead in the middle of our waiting periods in life.

One definition of *resurrection* that doesn't specifically have to do with the second coming of Christ is "coming back to life." I'm not sure about you, but there have been times in my life where I was in a period of waiting and felt like all life had been sucked from me. I was in need of resurrection. One such time comes to mind first.

In our third adoption attempt, after two failed adoptions, Jared and I were in Ukraine, ready to take our daughter home. While we were there, she was taken from the orphanage by a man who had her out of the country in forty-eight hours. She wasn't just an idea of a child we would one day bring home; we had known her for a long time, we loved her, and we wanted her to be our daughter. For all intents and purposes, she *was* our daughter. This was the final trip to bring her home, and everything came crashing down.

It would take a while to sort out the details—long after I had washed back up on United States soil—but ultimately, we found out that she was taken by her uncle who had been told a lot of lies about us, and thus we were told a lot of lies about him. Beyond the complicated details, what matters for this story is the wake left in my husband's and my hearts. And even in our daughter's.

When a child is taken from you and you don't know where they are, your mind really has trouble moving on. I often think of families whose children were abducted or ran away. When your child is out there somewhere, but you don't know where, and you don't know if they're safe, your mind goes to the darkest of places. I understand why these parents never move on in their hope of seeing them again. And many of them never allow themselves to grieve, because that means there's an end without that beloved child. In reality, there is no way to put a period on the story or add a conclusion for someone to have closure.

When I came home from Ukraine, I had to grieve as if she had died. If we were going to move on and ever have any children, I had to find a way to grieve her. I had to reconcile that her life was not meant to be a part of ours and that I would never see her again.

I was standing, waiting for Jesus just like Mary and Martha were in this next story. And while they hoped for a physical resurrection, I was looking for my *soul* to come back to life.

We find Jesus in John 11 hearing of his friend Lazarus dying. Jesus was good friends with Lazarus and his two sisters, Mary and Martha. His relationship with them shows up quite a few times in the Bible, which leads us to believe He had a special friendship with them.

Jesus was asked to come back to Judea by Mary and Martha to "wake" Lazarus. A little confusion ensued when He told the disciples He needed to go back to Judea because Lazarus had "fallen asleep." The disciples didn't want him to go. Judea wasn't safe at that moment because Jesus had made many enemies there (see John 10). And furthermore, if Lazarus was just asleep because he was sick, he would eventually wake up, and he certainly didn't need Jesus's help to do that. Jesus finally explained that Lazarus was dead, and that they must go to him, which was when the disciples followed Him to Judea.

Thomas, one of the disciples, followed the exchange with, "Let us also go, that we may die with him" (John 11:16). What Thomas meant was because of the danger in Judea and the people looking to kill Jesus, they might encounter trouble, and if they did, he was willing to die with Jesus. Thomas exhibited immense trust and faith in the Lord and His purposes.

What follows is what I believe to be one of the most important parts of scripture you will ever read. Four days after Mary and Martha's brother died, Jesus arrived on the scene:

> *Martha said to Jesus, "Lord, if you had been here, my brother would not have died. But even now I know that whatever you ask from God, God will give you." Jesus said to her, "Your brother will rise again." Martha said to him, "I know that he will rise again in the resurrection on the last day." Jesus said to her, "I am the resurrection and the life. Whoever believes in me, though he die, yet shall he live, and everyone who lives and believes in me shall never die. Do you believe this?" She said to him, "Yes, Lord; I believe that you are the Christ, the Son of God, who is coming into the world."*
>
> *(John 11:21–27)*

Jesus showed up four days after Lazarus passed away. If He was going to show up at all, why would He make Mary and Martha wait four days?

Expecting God

As I have mentioned before in this book, not all waiting periods are long. We've explored some that lasted literal lifetimes (Sarah waiting ninety-nine years before she became a mom), but some, like this one, are short in comparison. But time moves differently in the waiting after a tragedy, especially when waiting for a miracle. Each day likely felt like ninety-nine years to Mary and Martha.

After Martha saw Jesus, she first accused Him, saying that had he been there earlier, Lazarus would have never died. She automatically thought He would have jumped in to intervene and this never would have happened. Have you ever thought that? *God, if you had shown up sooner, this wouldn't have happened. So-and-so wouldn't have died, I wouldn't have lost my job, we wouldn't have lost our home, my child wouldn't be sick, etc. If Jesus had intervened sooner, maybe this heartache wouldn't have happened.*

I have felt this in my experience a million times over. I have memory of a day—but it may very well have been a collection of days—where the curtains were drawn in our

bedroom, and I was crying in our bed. Sobbing. I tried
to get up to go open the curtains to let some light in, and
I fell on the ground weeping. I could not reconcile what
had happened to me and to our little girl with the God I
knew. Didn't He call us to adopt? Didn't He guide our way
to her? Wasn't this His voice I had been following? What
kind of God would allow this
to happen? *Where was He?*

I had never, in my whole
entire life, questioned Him
the way I did then. For a girl
so full of faith, for the first
time, I was losing mine. I was
just like Martha, only able to
see a little bit of the picture.
Jesus is Lord all the time,
no matter how or when He
chooses to show up. And this was precisely the point He
was making here.

> Maybe His power
> could be shown
> through stopping
> an event, but
> how much more
> is His power on
> display when He
> reverses an event
> mankind can't
> touch?

Not even death can overthrow God's timing. Maybe
His power could be shown through stopping an event,
but how much more is His power on display when He
reverses an event mankind can't touch?

The part of the Bible I mentioned earlier that I
believe is one of the most important moments in history

is when Martha and Jesus had an exchange about the resurrection.

Jesus said, "Your brother will rise again" (John 11:23).

To which Martha replied, "I know that he will rise again in the resurrection on the last day" (John 11:24).

Martha named a place and a time that is unknown to us all as something that God has promised will happen; a time when the Messiah will return for His people and the "dead in Christ shall rise again."

For the Lord himself will descend from heaven with a cry of command, with the voice of an archangel, and with the sound of the trumpet of God. And the dead in Christ will rise first. Then we who are alive, who are left, will be caught up together with them in the clouds to meet the Lord in the air, and so we will always be with the Lord.

(1 Thessalonians 4:16–17)

This is the promise of His second coming, when Martha knew she would see her loved ones again who had died. She was now sadly attributing this to her brother, Lazarus.

Martha was looking for an end. A time when her sorrow would be no more. A time when she would no longer be waiting to see her brother again. A time when "resurrection" would be defined and would mean something. But Martha's mistake was looking for an *end* rather than looking for *Jesus*.

Jesus replied to Martha, "I am the resurrection and the life" (John 11:25).

This moment in scripture is the thunderbolt moment for me. I imagine the ground shook beneath Martha and she got chills all over her body. She had been looking for an end to this waiting, which she could only define as the place of resurrection, when the whole time she should have been looking for the *Who* of the resurrection.

After months of questioning the Lord when we lost our little girl, I had this exact moment one day in that same bedroom, on that same tear-stained carpet. His peace thundered in my heart, and I realized there would be no physical resurrection. She wasn't coming back, and He wasn't reversing what had happened to us. But He was the life I was looking for. He could resurrect my broken heart to love again. He could pull me together and breathe life into my mind and my bones so that He could begin a new work in and through me. It took some time, but I finally saw the *Who* of the resurrection again.

Friend, if you are waiting for the life that has been drained from you to come rushing back, stop looking for a *moment in time* and start looking for *Him*. His whole reason in coming to this earth and wanting a relationship with you is to bring life eternal.

Jesus followed up His thunderbolt sentence with, "Whoever believes in me, though he die, yet shall he live, and everyone who lives and believes in me shall never die. Do you believe this?" (John 11:25–26).

He was trying to show Martha several things. First, though Lazarus was dead, not only would he be alive in the resurrection because of his belief in Jesus, yes, but he was alive in spirit *at that moment* because he believed in Jesus. He would never die, because he was a believer. And second, Jesus was foreshadowing the power of His presence. His presence was life. His showing up on the scene brought resurrection because the resurrection was not a *destination*, it was *Him*.

I know your waiting season has sucked the life from you. I know you feel drained and, quite frankly, dead, most days. But, friend, look to God because not only does He *bring* life, He *is* life.

He may not take the waiting away. He may not end it when you want. But if you have Him, you have life. And *this* life is the life of abundance.

Let's look at how God revealed himself through Mary, Martha, and Lazarus's story.

God's Purpose in the Resurrection

Mary and Martha, and all the people present that day, knew that Jesus could have stopped Lazarus's death from happening. We've already reviewed Martha's accusation in John 11:21. Mary and a crowd of people present both repeated the sentiment. The crowd said, "Could not he who opened the eyes of the blind man also have kept this man from dying?" (John 11:37).

When God is taking you through a season of waiting for resurrection, the main purpose I see is to show His power to you and to those around you.

We often read these accusatory verses from Mary and Martha, and those present that day, in a negative light. However, what I notice about each of these statements is their *acknowledgement* of Him as Lord. Both Mary and Martha addressed Him as "Lord." Mary even fell at Jesus's feet when she came up to Him, a sign of acknowledging Him as a deity. And the crowd, they acknowledged His power when they referenced another miracle He had done, healing the blind man. They knew His power. They knew His magnificence.

The Lord was going to show them all something that day, something that He would choose not to continue to show on earth as a regular occurrence.

When Jesus said to Martha in John 11:25, "I am the resurrection and the life. Whoever believes in me, though he die, yet shall he live," He was trying to point her eyes to heaven and what the meaning of heaven really is.

But on that recorded day in history, He brought heaven to earth. He showed Martha, Mary, and those gathered that day just who He really was. There was no denial.

John 11:38–44 gives us the scene we've been waiting for:

Then Jesus, deeply moved again, came to the tomb. It was a cave, and a stone lay against it. Jesus said,

"Take away the stone." Martha, the sister of the dead man, said to him, "Lord, by this time there will be an odor, for he has been dead four days." Jesus said to her, "Did I not tell you that if you believed you would see the glory of God?" So they took away the stone. And Jesus lifted up his eyes and said, "Father, I thank you that you have heard me. I knew that you always hear me, but I said this on account of the people standing around, that they may believe that you sent me." When he had said these things, he cried out with a loud voice, "Lazarus, come out." The man who had died came out, his hands and feet bound with linen strips, and his face wrapped with a cloth. Jesus said to them, "Unbind him, and let him go."

Jesus showed His majesty and pointed everyone's eyes and hearts up toward heaven as He thanked God for performing the miracle. This was how everyone there would know that Jesus was who He said He was—*the* resurrection. This was proof that the resurrection was a person and not a place and time.

Lazarus was bound with linen strips, and later in John, we find out what these strips were all about, when Jesus died.

After these things Joseph of Arimathea, who was a disciple of Jesus, but secretly for fear of the Jews, asked Pilate that he might take away the body of Jesus, and Pilate gave him permission. So he came and took away his body. Nicodemus also, who earlier had come to Jesus by night, came bringing a mixture of myrrh and aloes, about seventy-five pounds in weight. So they took the body of Jesus and bound it in linen cloths with the spices, as is the burial custom of the Jews.

(John 19:38–40)

Because of this description later, we can assume this is what John 11:44 means when it mentions Lazarus's linen strips. He was likely buried with the same customary attention. These strips, over time, became known as "grave clothes."

Jesus then asked those present to unbind Lazarus. You know what happens when the waiting is over and resurrection comes? You no longer need grave clothes. You are unbound. Nothing can hold you down. The strips bound around Lazarus to preserve him in death were no longer useful.

You may not recognize them as this, but you have grave clothes too. The sweats you have kept on for days on end because "Why get dressed if I am depressed?" The T-shirt you've worn for weeks because you can't get out of bed. And even if it's not literal clothing, you have figurative grave clothes of unbelief and sadness covering your spirit and mind.

When Jesus asked to roll away the stone over Lazarus's tomb, Martha said, "Lord, by this time there will be an odor, for he has been dead four days" (John 11:39). Just like Lazarus, you aren't really living, and you smell like it.

When we are in the time of waiting for resurrection, we smell like death. And while we may not see a physical example in front of our faces like the people did the day Lazarus was raised from the dead, Jesus longs to resurrect us. Not only does He long to show us the life we have in Him in the here and now, He also longs for us to be with Him when the final resurrection comes.

As he said to Martha, "Do you believe this?" (John 11:26).

159

The purpose in waiting for resurrection is so the Lord can show you *who* He is. Believe in Him. Take off your grave clothes. Smell no more. Receive the life He is freely giving. He is the resurrection you've been waiting for.

LESSONS ON LOVING
IN THE WAITING

*What I have realized is that we can all love one
another better in our waiting periods.*

*When a friend is waiting for God to speak, to direct
them, or to give them something—we can be God's
arms of peace on this earth for them.*

You have no idea how painful their waiting period is.
Step in and help them breathe through it.
                              —Me, a blog posted on June 9, 2017[19]

I love ending this book with the story of Jesus and
Lazarus. They were genuine friends. They had experienced life together. Then Jesus was present for one of the
darkest moments in Lazarus's family's life.

The lessons the Lord teaches us in this story are the
exact things we should do for those we love who are in the
waiting right now.

However, this is twofold. If *you* are in the waiting period
right now, you can instruct those closest to you to love you

this way. But also, if you're not right now in the waiting but *someone you love* is, you can reference this list for how to show up and love them best. Jesus's lessons in John 11 are good fodder for the journey, no matter where you are.

Jesus didn't go to Mary and Martha's side right away when He knew of Lazarus's death. If you read John 11:6, you'll find that it says Jesus stayed where He was for two more days. Not because He didn't care, but because He was all about the timing, and He needed to finish the work where He was first.

Lessons from Jesus in this story to consider:

1. When a loved one is hurting, *go to them when the time is right*—for you and for them.

    One of the things that has been most difficult for me in my time of life right now (thirty-six years old, a wife, and a mom of three small kiddos) is that I cannot drop all I'm doing to show up for everyone as soon as they need me. The people who need me most every day, my husband and boys, get the "first parts" of me. The rest of me is what everyone else gets. And that's sucky. It just is.

    I'm going to be honest: I've had moments along this journey of my son's brain tumor in which I've been upset when someone didn't show up right away. Just like Mary and Martha were. But then I think about that person I wanted to show up quicker, and you know what? They have a family who gets their "first parts." And that's how it should be.

The work you do at home is the most important work, so you have to take care of those things first, but *then* SHOW UP when it makes sense for you. That is the example Jesus gave us. He showed up when it was the right time and after He had taken care of the important work He was doing.

2. Once you show up, *be all there*.

When Jesus showed up on the scene, His only purpose was to be there for Mary and Martha and to raise Lazarus from the dead. He wasn't going to entertain anything else; He was there for them.

When you show up for your loved one in need, put your phone down. Fix your eyes on them, and clear your ears from all other noise so you can listen if they need to talk. Be there only for them in this moment.

3. *Grieve with them.*

John 11:35 has become one of the most famous verses of all time because of the brevity coupled with the emotion Jesus showed. In that moment, Jesus was human and felt just like Mary and Martha felt. John 11:35 says, "Jesus wept." He let His emotions flow so He could truly empathize and not just sympathize. *Mary and Martha didn't need Jesus's words; they needed His presence.*

When you are with your loved one who is chest deep in this waiting season, feel free to allow yourself to feel all the emotions with them. Silently cry, be a shoulder for their tears, or be an ear for their words. Let them feel in the space of your company and join them if you want to and can. Be a companion of silence when they need your presence more than anything else.

4. When the time is right, *help them remove their grave clothes.*

This may not happen in that moment when you are there for them. This moment may come hours or maybe even months later. When their waiting period is over, or they are moving to a new phase, help them take their grave clothes off. Help them see that they no longer need these strips of their past and reminders of their death. Help them see the abundant life that God has created for them and cheer them on to live in it.

This list is full of all the things I wish my family and friends knew when I was in one of the longest waiting seasons of my life, the season of adopting our first child. People were loving on me from corners where they could, but there was something missing. Waiting to adopt a child isn't a path that has a clear, linear guide. There was no set time for when my child would come home.

I remember when I reached the eight- and nine-month marks of waiting to bring our first child home. When these monthly markers came around, I remember looking down at my belly and wailing. Normally, a pregnant woman would be preparing for birth, but there I was, with no physical evidence that I had "carried" and loved a child for nine months. I felt excruciatingly barren.

I would end up waiting two years and ten months, and losing three individual adoptions, before I ever brought my first babe home. I was "paper pregnant" for the length of nearly four pregnancies. That waiting season was the most difficult for me, and because it wasn't a traditional waiting season of being pregnant, people couldn't show up for me in a "normal" way.

I wish this list had existed for those in my life back then, so they could have known how to love me better, how to love me in my waiting.

I know whatever season of waiting you are in is coming to mind as you read this. You know what you need from your community and from the Lord. Petition Him now, and be encouraged by the stories you've read throughout this book.

- Stand firm in your faith like Noah. Know that you will not perish during this tumultuous time.

- Be patient like Abraham and Joseph. Know that the best of God's blessings for you are yet to come.

- Be faithful like Jacob and Moses. Continue about the things God has called you to do during this season.

- Be courageous like David and Daniel. Know that the Lord is giving you strength for this arduous journey.

- Be prayerful like Job and Habakkuk. Know that God longs most of all to be in relationship with you. Now, more than ever, you have the time to be in constant communion with Him.

- And finally, recognize the Lord for who He is in the midst of your waiting, like Mary and Martha. He has your best interests at heart, and He longs to make His majesty and grandeur known through this stage of your life.

Wait for Him. His timing is impeccable. His promises are certain. His purpose is paramount. His presence is all-encompassing. And the love He has is abundant beyond measure. Trust His purpose while you wait for what comes next. Your destiny within God's kingdom is worth the wait.

ACKNOWLEDGMENTS

I want to first thank my husband, Jared. You've carved space in our home for me to write and dream, and that will forever be the reason people will read what I write. Babe, you have believed in me and pushed me to follow my dreams of being an author from the first moment you knew that's what kept me up at night. Thank you for your love and for being a fan of who I am. I love you, and I like you.

To my kiddos, Aiden, Ryman, Tomlin, and the lil' boy we just found out will join us this year—you four boys have brought a richness to my life I never imagined possible. I didn't think I could love this much, laugh this much, or obsess as much over your little lives. I love when you learn something new and want to show me. I love when you hug me and tell me that you love me. I love reading to you and tucking you into bed. I am in complete awe that you are mine, and I will forever be thankful to be your mama.

To Mom, Dad, and Josh—thank you for all the years of togetherness. Our nomadic life was not for the faint of heart, but our motto was always that wherever the four of us were, that was home. No walls defined our home; we together were "home." This lesson has carried over into my own little family. The bond we share is surely attributed to the love and care you showed me my entire life. Josh, thank you for adding to this love fivefold with Lauren, Abigail, Anderson, Anna-Grace, and Athyns. I am so proud to be a part of your family and grateful to call you mine.

To my Ribbles—Reid, DeaNa, Clint, Rachel, Joseff, and Benjamin—thank you for supporting and loving our family and for letting me be one of you. I love being a Ribble.

To my dearest friend Casey—you have shown me for many years what waiting on the Lord, and doing so with grace, looks like. I know that your waiting times then, and even now, have not been easy. I want you to know that your life has been a sweet testament to God's goodness for me. I am forever grateful for you and your friendship.

Thank you Matt West and my Dexterity team. Matt, you took a chance on me, and I will forever be grateful for you making this gal's dreams come true. To my team there—you rock, and I am so thankful for all the work you've put into my book.

To my editors, Lauren and Kathryn—your voices make me better. Editing is not always fun, but the result is always wonderful. I am so thankful for both of you and the time you took to pore over my heart that was spread across these pages.

To my friend Kelsie, who has entered what appears to be a waiting season with no end. Please know you are seen, loved, known, and cherished. I know the Lord has you in His palm and cares for every single ounce of you. I love you, and I am always here for you. And when I forget to show up and just be silent with you in the tough stuff, tell me to shut up.

To the Gibbs and the Carpenter families—thank you for your friendship and for all the cheerleading both you and your parents have done with my writing. The support means the world to me.

NOTES

EPIGRAPH

1. Morgan Harper Nichols (@morganharpernichols), "For the waiting," Instagram photo, September 18, 2020, https://www.instagram.com/p/CFS-8sSgR3C/.

CHAPTER 1

2. National Geographic Staff, "Tornadoes, Explained," *National Geographic*, August 28, 2019, https://www.nationalgeographic.com/environment/natural-disasters/tornadoes/#close.

CHAPTER 2

3. Nancy Tillman, On the Night You Were Born (New York: Feiwel & Friends, 2005).
4. Jeremy Breland, "Abram to Abraham? Why Did He Do It?" Walterboro Live, June 28, 2020, https://walterborolive.com/stories/abram-to-abraham-why-did-he-do-it-faith,32425.
5. "Sarah, Sarai, Sara: The Woman Who Became Mother of Nations," Bible Gateway, https://www.biblegateway.com/resources/all-women-bible/Sarah-Sarai-Sara.

CHAPTER 3

6. Michael Bublé, "Haven't Met You Yet," by Amy Foster-Gillies and Alan Chang, October 9, 2009, *Crazy Love*, Reprise Records, compact disc.

CHAPTER 5

7. Lisa Appelo, "3 Truths When You're in the Wilderness," LisaAppelo.com, https://lisaappelo.com/3-truths-when-youre-in-the-wilderness/.
8. Steven Curtis Chapman, "The Great Adventure," June 19, 1992, The Great Adventure, Sparrow Records, compact disc.
9. Martin K.M.,"17 Things Joseph's Life Tells You About Your Dream and Purpose," Some Inspired Thoughts, September 13, 2018, https://www.someinspiredthoughts.com /17-things -josephs-life-tells-you-about-your-dream-and-purpose/.

CHAPTER 6

10. Anonymous, often attributed to Mark Twain.
11. Christine Caine, "Embrace Your Place," Facebook video, October 27, 2020, https://www.facebook.com/watch/?v=3636 35635084281.

CHAPTER 7

12. Henrietta Mears, What the Bible Is All About (Carol Stream, IL: Tyndale House Publishers, 2016), 210.

CHAPTER 8

13. Jon Acuff, "The Truth About Callings," *Stuff Christians Like* (blog), November 17, 2013, http://stuffchristianslike.net/2013 /11/17/truth-callings/.

CHAPTER 9

14. John Mayer, "Waiting on the World to Change," by John Mayer and Stephen Jordan, July 11, 2006, Continuum, Aware Records, compact disc.
15. "Introduction to Habakkuk," ESV.org, https://www.esv.org /resources/esv-global-study-bible/introduction-to-habakkuk/.
16. Intl Justice Mission (@IJM), "'God has a plan to help bring justice to the world—and his plan is us.'—Gary Haugen," Twitter, February 27, 2017, 9:04 a.m., https://twitter.com/IJM /status/836230425743872003.
17. Anonymous, often attributed to Oscar Wilde.

CHAPTER 10

18. Wikipedia, s.v. "Do Not Stand at My Grave and Weep," last modified January 28, 2021, https://en.wikipedia.org/wiki/Do _Not_Stand_at_My_Grave_and_Weep.

LESSONS ON LOVING IN THE WAITING

19. Krystal Ribble, "Love Me in the Waiting," Krystal Ribble (blog), June 9, 2017, http://www.krystalribble.com/love-me-in -the-waiting/.

ABOUT THE AUTHOR

Krystal Ribble is a freelance writer and author of *The Church's Orphans*. She aims to breathe new life into and bring a modern understanding to the stories we've read about in the Bible all our lives, showing readers how those stories are still relevant today. Her writing builds on experiences mentoring college-aged students and advocating for orphans and vulnerable children across the United States.

Krystal earned a Bachelor of Science in Gerontology and Health Care Management from North Greenville University and Master of Arts in Christian Leadership from Liberty Baptist Theological Seminary and Graduate School. She now lives in Nashville, Tennessee with her husband, Jared, and their three boys. *Love Me in the Waiting* is Krystal's second book.

Connect with Krystal
on her blog and socials

🌐 krystalribble.com
📷 @krystalribble
📘 @krystalmribble